P9-AGV-024

AMERICAN
ART DECO
ARCHITECTURE AND REGIONALISM

CARLA BREEZE

PHOTOGRAPHY BY CARLA BREEZE

W. W. NORTON & COMPANY • NEW YORK • LONDON

DEDICATED TO THE MEMORY OF DAVID GEBHARD

Printed in Italy
First Edition

The text of this book is composed in Eagle, designed in 1933 by Morris Fuller Benton (1872–1948) for the National Recovery Administration. A digitized version was prepared in 1994 by David Berlow and Jonathan Corum for the Font Bureau. The display type, Parisian, was designed by Benton in 1928 for the American Type Founders Company.

Manufacturing by Mondadori Printing, Verona

Book design by Robert L. Wiser, Silver Spring, Maryland

Endpapers. Dupont Building, 169 East Flagler, Miami, Florida, 1937–38. Marsh & Saxelbye, architects.

Page 1. Texas Centennial Exposition Buildings, Fair Park, Dallas, Texas. 1935–36. George L. Dahl and Donald Nelson, architects; gold medallion bas-relief designed by Joseph C. Renier.

Page 2. Cities Service Building (AIG), 70 Pine Street, New York, New York, 1932. Clinton & Russell and Holton & George, architects.

Page 5 (opposite). Paramount Theater (Paramount Arts Center), 23 East Galena Boulevard, Aurora, Illinois, 1931, Rapp & Rapp, architects.

Library of Congress Cataloging-in-Publication Data
Breeze, Carla
American art deco : architecture and regionalism / by Carla Breeze.
p. cm.
Includes bibliographical references and index.
ISBN 0-393-01970-5
1. Art deco (Architecture)—United States. I. Title.
NA712.5.A7 B698 2003
720'.973'09042—dc21 2002025474

W.W. Norton & Company, Inc., 500 Fifth Avenue, New York, N.Y. 10110
www.wwnorton.com

W.W. Norton & Company Ltd., Castle House, 75/76 Wells Street, London W1T 3QT

1 2 3 4 5 6 7 8 9 0

ABUNDANCE
AGRI CULT URE

CONTENTS

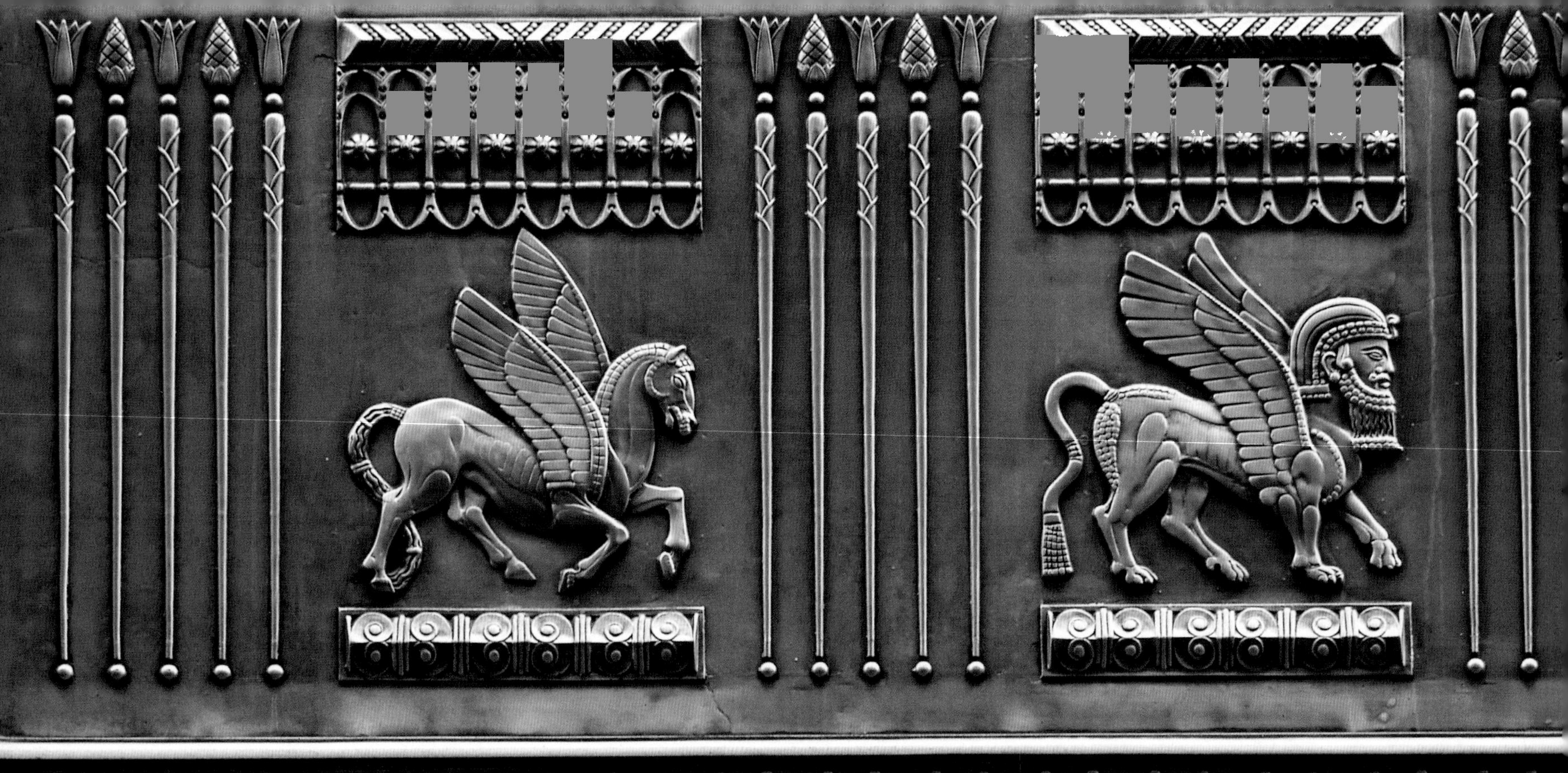
THE FREN

PREFACE

Art deco architecture flourished in large cities and small towns throughout America in the 1920s and 1930s. Extremely popular as a statement of twentieth-century modernity and technological progress, art deco movie palaces, dime stores, department stores, courthouses, and schools became ubiquitous in the American landscape. Consequently, art deco is one of the few styles of architecture that the majority of Americans can easily identify. Art deco structures are frequently listed on national, state, and local historic registers. Regrettably, these factors have not always resulted in broad support for the style's preservation and maintenance of architectural integrity. As decorative arts from the 1920s and 1930s have become highly desirable and eagerly sought by connoisseurs and collectors, the dismemberment of art deco buildings has occurred, providing decorative elements to be sold on the private market.[1] Due to the extreme value of chandeliers, light fixtures, metalwork, glass, and other decorative elements, removal of these components continues, depriving art deco buildings of the integral features which define the style.

The buildings featured in *American Deco* are those which have maximum architectural integrity: exterior features, such as windows, doors, light fixtures, and ornament, and interior ceilings, elevator doors, stairways, and decorative ornament, have not been drastically altered or removed. Buildings from the 1920s and 1930s in the art deco style which have not been modified are rare. A majority of art deco buildings were commercial, and have been prey to considerations of profit and convenience. Interior spaces are especially vulnerable to modifications resulting from upgraded building codes, maintenance issues, and even changing aesthetics. Other losses result from misguided judgment, such as the replacement of bronze grille doors or the modification of illumination.[2] (Since original light levels were lower than is currently acceptable, this is a major cause of remodeling.) These factors have had a grave impact on architectural preservation. Numerous other buildings that might have been included in *American Deco* were undergoing restoration while this project was being completed.

Commercial architecture is especially vulnerable to market forces and changes in technology. My survey of art deco buildings conducted over the past eleven years indicates that buildings which are owned by one person or a small group of private owners tend to be scrupulously maintained compared to those owned by larger real estate entities, although there are exceptions—corporations which do recognize the historic value of their properties. Private owners, however, are essentially collectors of a large and expensive medium who understand the significance of maintaining the architectural integrity of their buildings. Maintenance and preservation are costly, but without such collectors, the unique characteristics of numerous buildings would be eroded. The Stock Exchange Lunch Club (now the City Club) in San Francisco, owned by The Empire Group; Naniboujou Lodge in Minnesota, owned by Tim and Nancy Raney; and the Edgar Miller complexes in Chicago, owned by Mark C. Mamolen of Carl Street Partners are particularly significant because even the original furniture remains in these notable buildings. Corporate entities, as well, are certainly capable of maintaining their interiors (in general, primarily lobbies), as exemplified by AIC's Cities Service Building. Theaters have fared better than other types of commercial buildings, since many are managed by nonprofit agencies or civic organizations. The Paramount Theatre in Oakland was acquired by the Oakland Symphony in 1972, and contains original furniture and fixtures, which have been meticulously conserved. Due to the devoted efforts of local preservationists, the Egyptian Theater in Atlanta was saved with virtually every piece of furniture intact when it was scheduled to be demolished. Art deco societies and other preservation organizations in the major cities and various regions of the United States have contributed to public appreciation and preservation of buildings from this period.

Fred F. French Building, 551 Fifth Avenue, New York, New York, 1927, H. Douglas Ives (in-house architect for the French Company) with John Sloan of Sloan & Robertson, architects.

ACKNOWLEDGMENTS

James L. Mairs, senior editor at W. W. Norton, suggested the concept of photographing notable art deco buildings in as much detail as possible. This approach offered me an opportunity to document buildings in various regions of the United States where I had not worked previously, and ultimately to preserve examples of art deco for future generations. A substantial portion of the work in *American Deco* is the result of an individual research grant from the Design Division of the National Endowment for the Arts to survey and photograph art deco architecture in the Midwest and Prairie region.

American Deco: Architecture and Regionalism would not have been feasible without the efforts and contributions of numerous individuals, corporations, and public institutions. I would like to express appreciation to Phillip de Capua, property manager for Shorenstein Real Estate of the Fred F. French Building; Hector L. Diaz, county clerk for the Bronx County Courthouse; Maurice R. Greenberg, president and CEO of AIG, Cities Service Building; Fred Wunschel, Gerard Dengel, and Jason Knoblock of AIG; Mark Heutlinger, administrator, and Elka Deitsch, senior curator, of the Herbert and Eileen Bernard Museum; Reva Kirschberg, curator emeritus, at Congregation Emanu-El; Monsignor Stafford of the Church of the Most Precious Blood; Monsignor Grace of St. Andrew Avalino Church; David Panzirer of 275 Madison Avenue; Stephen Klein of the Fuller Building; William J. Henderson, postmaster general of the United States Postal Service; Anthony Masiello, mayor of Buffalo, and Richard Sacco, Buffalo City Hall; William E. Davis and Mark D. Frank of Niagara Mohawk Power Corporation; Joseph Bogansky, Integrity Trust Building; David Adamancy, president of Temple University; Eugene Hickock, secretary of education, Commonwealth of Pennsylvania; Gary D. Wolfe, deputy secretary of education, Commonwealth of Pennsylvania; Monsignor Shuda of Our Lady of Perpetual Help; David Newcome, B. F. Saul Company for Kennedy-Warren Apartments; M. J. Foster, governor of Louisiana, and Sammie Cockrell, executive assistant to clerk, Sylvia Breaux, Louisiana State Capitol; Bill Tharpe, director of archives, Reggie Eady, Property Services, and Sharon Stephens, Alabama Power Company; Wendy Rigg of Fox Theatre, Atlanta; Jeff Lehman of the National Hotel; James L. Westbrook, Jr., city manager of Asheville, North Carolina; Maggie O'Connor, City of Asheville; Paul D. Tonti, Gary Worthy, Patricia Boyle, and Diane Moore of the Smith Group (Guardian Trust Building); Amy Messano of Michcon (Guardian Trust Building); Reverend Monsignor William H. Easton, National Shrine of the Little Flower; Ray Bean, AIA, National Shrine of the Little Flower; Robert B. Jones, mayor of Kalamazoo; Dr. Gerhardt Knoedle, director, Cranbrook Academy of Art; Claudia Lord, Joe Keaty, and John McDonald, Mark IV Realty Group, Union Carbide and Carbon Building; Mark C. Mamolen, Carl Street Partners; David Brennan, chairman, Chicago Board of Trade; Ron Patten, superintendent, and Robert Krueger, principal, Bloom High School; Julie Jung, Mundelein College; William Mason, general director, and Ken Shaw, facilities director, Chicago Lyric Opera; Anne K. Hughes, and Julie A. Nowak, Equity, Lyric Opera Office Building; David Stover, mayor of Aurora, Illinois; Charles Blair, director, Madame Walker Theatre Center; James Quinn, Circle Tower; Michael J. Helak, market president, Firstar (Valley National Bank Building); Tracy Sweet, Charles Theater; Tim and Nancy Raney of Naniboujou Lodge; Mike Johanns, governor of Nebraska, Robert C. Ripley, manager of restoration, Roxanne Smith, and Gloria Witherspoon, Nebraska State Capitol Building; Linda Rajcevich and Jackie Thorstad of Joslyn Memorial Art Museum; Kay Barnes, mayor of Kansas City, Missouri; Diane Davis, Winbury Group, Kansas City Power & Light Building; Robert J. Marin and Roel Quintanilla, Wichita North High School; Roger L. Hinshaw and Marlin J. Miller, United States Federal Courthouse, Wichita; Henry Lussy, Washoe Theater; Dr. Mouzon Biggs, Jr., and Sherry Goodwin, Boston Avenue Methodist Church; Nora Cook and Dr. Laverne Ford Wimberly, Will Rogers High School; David R. Smith and J. W. Brown, Maricopa County Courthouse; Dennis Miller, Union Pacific Railroad, Texas & Pacific Passenger Terminal; Bob Terrell, city manager, Will Rogers Memorial Auditorium; Honorable T. Biscoe, Travis County Courthouse; Billy Delbert, Avalon Casino; Rabbi Harvey J. Fields and Stephen E. Bruer, Wilshire Boulevard Temple; Chavi Hertz, Park Plaza; Dr. E. C. Krupp, director, Griffith Observatory; Celeste Hong and Roger S. Hong, AIA, You Chung Hong Building, Forbidden City, and Roger Hong Gallery Building; Scott Field, AIA, Parkinson Archives; Anthony Nicco and Karen Collingwood, Chandler Properties, 1895 Pacific; Susan Murannishi, county administrator, and Michelle Fadelli, Alameda County Courthouse; Louise H.

Circle Tower, 5 East Market Street, Indianapolis, Indiana,
1928–29, Rubush & Hunter, architects.
Transom grille above Circle Tower's entrance.

Meiere Dunn; Merle O'Keeffe, Trish and Bruce Moxon, Joyce B. Gibson, and Marcelina Calabaza; Michele Schuff, restoration artist, the Fox Theatre, Atlanta; Steve Seaver, general manager, and Susan Santiago, property manager, Shell Building; Tracy D. Morgan, general manager, MB Beitler, One North LaSalle Street; R. J. Bellanca, manager, and Charles Clark, the City Club; Leslee Stewart and Ken Walters, docent, Paramount Theatre of the Arts, Oakland, California; Marina Baktis, manager, the Oviatt Building; Gary Duloc, Touches of Illusion, Inc.; Elizabeth Bowman, marketing manager, and Bill Langley, deputy director, Convention and Entertainment Centers (Kansas City Municipal Auditorium), Kansas City, Missouri; Karen Wagner, capitol archivist, State Building Division, Nebraska; Michelle Barber, event manager, Wiltern Theater; Leisanne Ontario, property manager, the Wiltern Center; Waldo T. Griego, property manager, GSA, Albuquerque District, New Mexico; Julius Decker, AMR Corporation, Jeff Hirsch, Allan Weitz, and Tommy Arce of Fotocare; Laurence Levine, Esq., Beldock, Levine and Hoffman; Wayne Decker; Billy Hassell, facility manager, Jefferson County Courthouse, Birmingham, Alabama; Shelly Kleppsattel, Atlanta Fox, PR, Joe Russo, PR, Niagara Mohawk; Tom Bean, city architect, Kansas City, Missouri; Oscar at the Albion Hotel; Anne Gould Hauberg; Turner Company, Detroit; Morrison, Morrison Finley, Detroit; Eric Mundell, reference services, Indiana Historical Society; Turner Company, Detroit; Cathy Johnstone, technical director, Jennifer Rice, public relations manager, The 5th Avenue Theatre; Roma A. Peyser, program director and Sydney Baer, Congregation Beth Israel; Robert L. Wiser, Catherine Osborne, and the Honorable Jerrold Nadler and staff.

TRANSP
RTATION
ABUNDANCE
AGRI
CULT
URE

INTRODUCTION

While the art deco style in the United States certainly gained momentum from the 1925 *Exposition Internationale des Arts Décoratifs et Industriels Modernes* in Paris, its origins are equally indebted to the avant-garde architects and philosophies of design which had existed in this country since the late nineteenth century. These architects and philosophies included the Arts and Crafts Movement; the Prairie School, exemplified by Frank Lloyd Wright's work; and architects such as Irving Gill on the West Coast and Robert D. Kohn in New York City, who promoted "modernity" as a moral mandate.[3] Additionally, architects in the Americas were able to delve into vast resources of pre-Columbian and historic indigenous cultures for inspiration and exotic motifs, a feature of early twentieth-century architecture that expressed a desire to break with past formulaic styles. Native American arts were geometric and highly stylized. Textiles produced by Navajo (*Dinah*), Hopi pottery, and other forms of Native American art became widely appreciated by artists and architects associated with the Arts and Crafts Movement, which also relied on geometric ornament.[4] Frank Lloyd Wright and architects associated with the Prairie School, too, were inspired by indigenous cultures. Wright designed the 1924 Nakota Country Club (an unbuilt project) with tipi-form buildings and envisioned large-scale sculptures of a Plains chief and woman flanking the entrance.[5]

Each region of America has a unique history and environment that shaped the vision of architects and designers in the 1920s and 1930s. Motifs for art deco ornament were frequently inspired by regional flora and fauna, local history, and traditional building styles. Spanish Colonial architecture was popular in Florida and the West, Sioux and Mandan wigwams probably influenced the Prairie School, and Anasazi complexes of irregular massing surfaced

St. Paul City Hall & Ramsey County Courthouse,
15 Kellogg Boulevard West, St. Paul, Minnesota, 1931–32,
Holabird & Root, architects with Ellerbe & Company;
Lee Lawrie, sculptor.

in the Pueblo revival style in the Southwest. The KiMo Theater in Albuquerque, New Mexico, resembles an adobe structure, and the ornament specifically refers to Pueblos along the Rio Grande. Waves and lush foliation are major components of art deco motifs in California. Magnolia and pelican motifs ornament the Louisiana State Capitol Building. Art deco's emphasis on industrial production and schematized, ethnic motifs was easily adapted to regionalism in America, and exoticism was provided by indigenous cultures. Mesoamerican archaeology had revealed astonishingly sophisticated cities with lavishly ornamented pyramids; Mayan motifs and architecture influenced, among others, Timothy L. Pflueger's 450 Sutter Street building in San Francisco and Robert Stacy-Judd's designs in Southern California.

By the turn of the twentieth century, popular culture regarded images of the Native American (or Indian) and related historical events as ideal symbols of American, not just regional, identity. Sculptors and other artists believed that the Indian's relationship to nature offered an alternative (and antidote) to rapid industrialization and urbanization.[6] Herman Lee Meader's 1914 Cliff Dweller apartment building, on Riverside Drive in New York City, provides one of the earliest extant examples of the use of Native American motifs (aside from exposition architecture) occurring outside the Southwest. Mountain lions alternate with Mesoamerican masks in a frieze which culminates in buffalo skulls at the corners of this modernistic building. Spandrels utilize the reversed swastika, a Navajo directional symbol. Another motif frequently associated with Native American design is the stepped diamond, a pattern which is woven into the brickwork of the Cliff Dweller apartments. On the West Coast, the 1927 Ahwahnee Hotel in Yosemite, California (designed by Gilbert Stanley Underwood, a nationally recognized hotel and railroad-terminal architect[7]) has stained-glass windows, terrazzo floors, ceilings, and furniture ornamented with motifs derived from native Pomo, Hupa, and Hurok basketry.[8]

Bassett Tower, 303 Texas Avenue, El Paso, Texas, 1930, Trost & Trost, architects. Bassett Tower illustrates the pervasiveness of the skyscraper form in all regions of the United States.

Native American culture was not the only source of inspiration for ornament. The sculptor of Mount Rushmore, John Gutzon Borglum, advocated the use of motifs derived from native flora and fauna because, he believed, they were more pertinent to contemporary design than antique devices such as the egg and dart.[9] Other artists also employed native motifs; for example, in 1930 the metalworker Nena de Brennecke described her use of Hopi symbols on the entrance grille of the Denver National Bank.[10] While other regional variants may not appear as distinct and widespread genres such as Pueblo deco, their local references give the buildings a distinction which is unrivaled by historical styles.[11] For example, the New York architect Elizabeth Coit, designer of the Walker-Gordon (milk) Company's interior, drew inspiration from the cattle and milk bottles of the upstate dairy industry.[12]

The frequent use of indigenous motifs was not without its dissenters. Barry Byrne, the Prairie School architect associated with numerous ecclesiastical commissions, had his own opinion on the value of regional ornament. Corresponding with Mark L. Peisch on June 8, 1955, "re: [George W.] Maher [a Prairie School architect]," he wrote: "a very pleasant, affable person, he had the courage normal to the successful American business type and a 'line' of talk which savored of self-advertising . . . superficial, non-basic ideas, that made 'copy' but actually were unimportant, like using the American thistle as a basic ornament. Nothing wrong with that but of questionable importance."[13] Byrne and architects of the Prairie School were involved with new concepts of plasticity and free-flowing floor plans, and applied ornament was viewed as superficial as the Prairie School evolved into modernism.

One industry which was particularly attentive to regionalism was communications. Writing about telephone building design for the April 1931 issue of *The Architectural Forum*, Charles G. Loring described American Telephone and Telegraph Company's (and its twenty-four subsidiaries in the United States) strategy for maintaining personal contact as the system became increasingly mechanized. "From the administration buildings occupying entire city

the diamond shop
Dr. Daniel J. Geller
OPTOMETRIST

Kogen-Miller Studios, 1734 Wells Street, Chicago, Illinois, 1928. Detail of stained glass made by Edgar Miller, portraying American wildlife, the raven and antelope.

blocks, down to the isolated toll-line repeater stations, the objective is to harmonize the design with the dominant native charcteristics." The article was illustrated by photographs of various Pacific Telephone and Telegraph Company buildings, including a pagoda for San Francisco's Chinatown and Mission style in Torrance and Ventura, California. Colonial façades were favored on the Atlantic seaboard.

The prevalence of stylized regional motifs in architecture during the 1920s and 1930s in the United States paralleled an increasing nationalism. An identical phenomenon, National Romanticism, was occurring abroad as democracies were formed in eastern and western European countries. Cubistic architecture in Czechoslovakia incorporated folk textile motifs, forms found in wooden vernacular buildings in the countryside, and images of Slovak warriors. Pavel Janák's interior of the Czech pavilion at the 1925 *Exposition Internationale des Arts Décoratifs et Industriels Modernes* featured a profusion of folk floral motifs on the coffered ceiling, and its leaded stained glass windows had geometric patterns derived from Slovakian embroidery.[14] Similar references to native folk arts were visible in the Polish National Pavilion. The Spanish National Pavilion featured *miradors,* corbels, and white stucco walls within a vaguely modernistic context. The exposition itself was originally impelled by nationalist sentiments—France reacting to the increasing dominance of German decorative arts as state institutions began to support industrial design and production.[15]

Nationalist attitudes in the United States encouraged the use of a theme which immigrants from diverse cultures could share—the indigenous Native American. Another factor also unified cultural diversity—modernism in architecture and consumer products. This emerging modern movement was a reaction to the *Ecole des Beaux-Arts.* Emphasizing function, natural materials, and integration of ornament, if any, modernism embodied the freedom of the New World, and these concepts began to suffuse every aspect of American life, from industry to philosophy. Thorstein Veblen's 1902 *Theory of the Leisure Class* criticized *Beaux-Arts* architecture for neglecting the simple beauty of vernacular forms.[16] Vernacular architecture is generally driven by function and available materials. Art deco cannot be considered vernacular, but it is populist, often simply a trenchant expression of *Beaux-Arts* classicism, which had thrived on double columns and figurative sculpture.[17] Modernism's impact on art deco was manifested in the use of geometric patterns, the exploitation of industrial materials for ornament, and bolder volumes. Architects and designers working in this new style considered their work to be *modernistic,* the term used during the 1920s and 1930s, which should not be confused with *modernism,* which evolved into the International style and similar modes. *Modernistic* is synonymous with the term art deco. Both are used in *American Art Deco.*

Architects working with artists was another feature of the *Beaux-Arts* ideal that lingered in art deco. Diverse artists such as Edgar Miller, Hildreth Meiere, Oscar B. Bach, and numerous other sculptors, metal workers, muralists and designers were crucial in the development and production of the ornament which essentially defines the art deco style. Modernistic embellishment was often produced using either new materials or new technologies. Linoleum, a material used for floor covering, was adapted by Pierre Bourdelle, who innovatively used the product to create murals. Industrial materials used extensively in art deco ornament and details included metal, concrete, and terra-cotta. Other traditional materials, for instance ceramic tile, were adapted to the angular, mechanized aesthetic simply by being mass-produced and modular. Eminent decorative artist Hildreth Meiere suggested that decoration during the 1920s was impelled by the plethora of "new materials, new metals, new structural materials, new fabrics, compounds, alloys and aggregates . . . while the old materials, such as glass, wood, ceramics, marble and established metals are being presented with new finishes, new properties, and new advantages."[18] Publications devoted to a particular material—such as *The Metal Arts, Stone*, and *Atlantic Terra Cotta*—were published to promote a specific product or industry. These journals offered technical information which would enable an architect or designer to specify a particular product for construction. In addition, advertising by manufacturers of materials increased substantially in professional journals during this period.

Mayan Theater, 1040 South Hill Street, Los Angeles, California, 1926–27, Morgan, Walls & Clements, architects. Cast concrete Mayan glyphs and warriors were sculpted by Francisco Coneja, originally the color of the material, gray.

METAL

In the early twentieth century, metal especially offered exciting potential; new alloys could be cast, extruded, welded, riveted, rolled, and drawn. *The Metal Arts* had a feature in every issue, "Drafting for Metal Work," which discussed and illustrated various aspects of different materials. For example, the first volume of *The Metal Arts* (November 1928) illustrated a building for the Commonwealth of Pennsylvania by Gehron, Roxx & Alley. The bronze entrance doors, the architect's rough sketch, a large-scale (one inch equals one foot) study, and C. Paul Jennewein's rough plastiline models for the panels (from which plaster casts were later made) elucidated the design and manufacturing process. The wood frame around the plastiline was an exact reproduction of the door's rails and stiles. The metalwork, cast by the Gorham Company in Rhode Island, was finished by hand with sharp steel tools, refining the work. *The Metal Arts* had another innovative feature: ideas and decorative concepts were disseminated via the "Portfolio" articles, which in this issue included the bronze entrance doors of the Canal Bank and Trust Company in New Orleans, Louisiana (Emile Weil, Inc., architect). The ornament on the rails and stiles of these doors was derived from animals and plants indigenous to America, especially Louisiana.[19]

Opposite. Oklahoma County Courthouse, 321 Park Avenue, Oklahoma City, Oklahoma, 1936–37, Solomon Layton, George Forsyth & Jewell Hicks, architects.

Top right. Wright's Trading Post, 616 Central SW, Albuquerque, New Mexico, c. 1935.

Bottom right. United States Courthouse, 501 Tenth Street, Fort Worth, Texas, 1933, Paul P. Cret, architect. Cast aluminum molding.

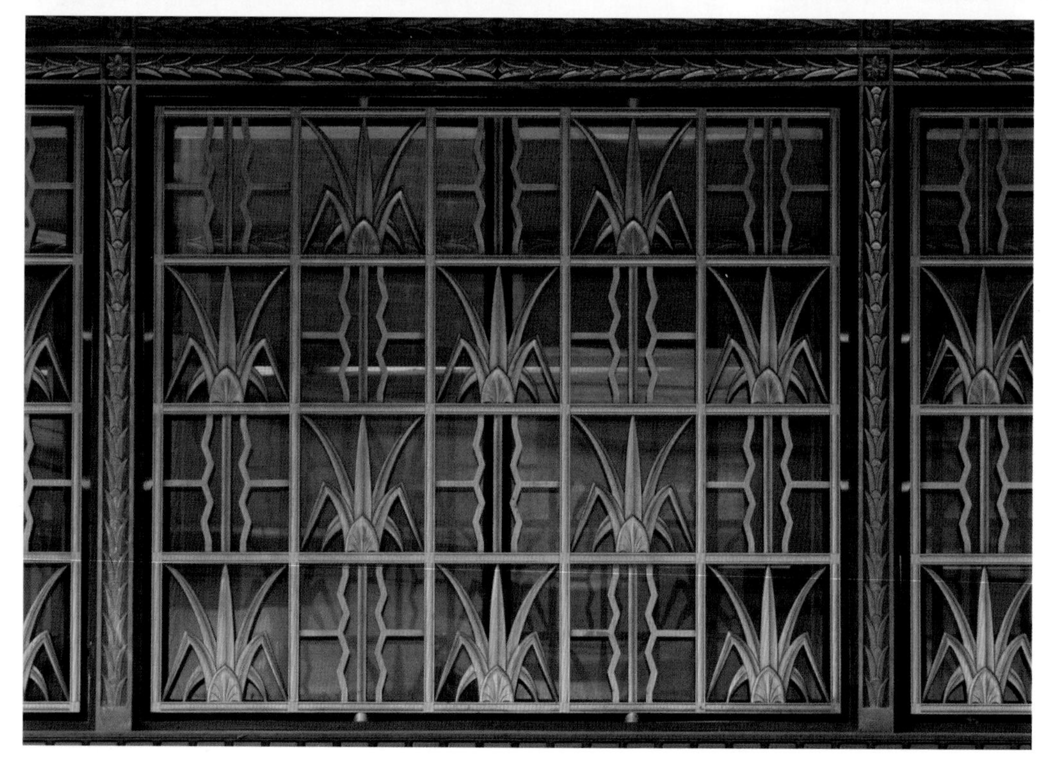

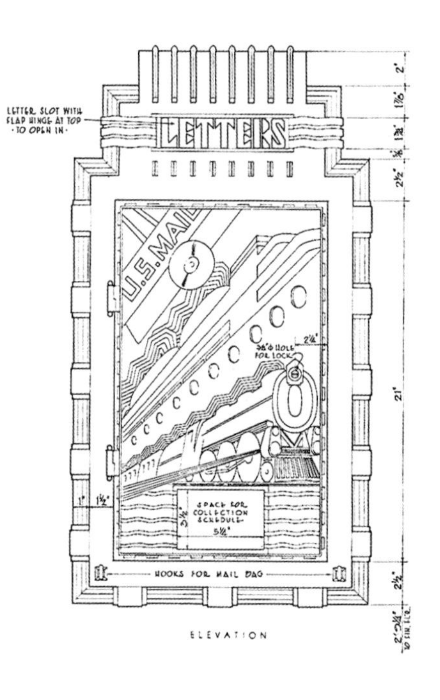

Top left. Goelet Building, 608 Fifth Avenue, New York, New York, 1932, E. H. Faile & Co., with Victor L. F. Hafner, was illustrated in *Architecture,* October 1934.

Top right. Goelet Building. Original interior of elevator cab.

Above left. Dupont Building, 169 East Flagler, Miami, Florida, 1937–38, Marsh & Saxelbye, architects.

Above right. 29 Broadway, New York, New York, Sloan & Roberts, architects. Drawing of lobby mailbox by J. C. Stewart.

Opposite. City Bank Farmers Trust, 22 William Street, New York, New York, 1931, Cross & Cross, architects.

HISTORICAL MUSEUM
HISTORICAL
MUSEUM

Top right. Tiffany Building, 727 Fifth Avenue, New York, New York, Cross & Cross, architects, 1940. Sculptor Henry F. Metzler carved "Atlas" from wood but painted it to resemble bronze. The sculpture dates from 1853 when it adorned the first Tiffany & Co. shop.

Opposite. St. Charles City Hall, 2 East Main Street, St. Charles, Illinois, 1935. Harold Zook, architect. Cast bronze foxes ornament the bridge across the Fox River, on the east bank of which City Hall is situated.

Bottom right. New York City Health Building, 2 Lafayette Street, New York, New York, 1935, Charles B. Meyers, architect.

CONCRETE

Cast concrete was the perfect medium for architectural ornament on buildings in which cost was a factor and was often utilized for modernistic decoration in California and the Southwest. Concrete was an ideal replacement for stone lintels and door surrounds, and was extensively used structurally and decoratively in California because it could be reinforced to withstand earthquakes. Ornamental elements for art deco were made using waste molds—plaster casts discarded after multiple use. Prior to the advent of modernistic design, these molds were employed to create elaborately detailed Spanish Colonial or Churrigueresque details, but when a design was simple and geometric without undercutting, wooden molds could be reused, reducing the cost of decoration. To some extent, this may explain why the Spanish Colonial revival was finally superseded by the modernistic style during the late 1920s in California.

Opposite top left. Blessed Sacrament Church, Thirty-fifth Avenue, Queens, New York, 1934–41, Henry J. McGill, architect.

Opposite top right. Pantages Theater, 6233 Hollywood Boulevard, Los Angeles, California, 1929, B. Marcus Pritecca, architect.

Opposite bottom left. The Elks Building (Park Plaza Hotel), 607 Park View Street, Los Angeles, California, 1924, Claude Beelman and William Curlett, architects. The Elks Building was published to illustrate the uses of concrete in *The Western Architect*, September 1927. Corner ornamentation is precast. The April 1926 *Architectural Record* also featured the building in "Portfolio: Current Architecture."

Opposite bottom right. Southern Pacific Train Station, Casa Grande, Arizona, 1940, William F. Meaney, architect. The station used an inexpensive technique for ornament—polychrome cement.

Left. Cliff Dweller Apartments, 243 Riverside Drive, New York, New York, 1914, Herman Lee Meader, architect.

PARK
PLAZA

TERRA-COTTA

Terra-cotta, a cast-clay product, was another relatively inexpensive decorative option, and one that offered innumerable possibilities for the use of color. It was less expensive than stone or other materials on which artists worked directly, because after a model was made, it could be reproduced mechanically, and endlessly. Costs were especially nominal if an architect worked with existing patterns designed by artists employed by the manufacturers. Even if elements were designed by the architect for a specific project, as many were, it was still economical because of mass-production techniques. Terra-cotta's ease of maintenance also made it appealing—it could simply be washed periodically with soap and water. But its most vital characteristic was certainly its association with rich color. Various regions favored specific colors. California architects used blue and green, the colors of the sea; New York City abounded with a multitude of colors to differentiate a building from surrounding structures and attract attention as a form of advertisement.

The industry magazine *Atlantic Terra Cotta* devoted its January 1928 issue to promoting the use of terra-cotta for smaller, less expensive buildings. Black and white photographs in the journal illustrate the uses of the Atlantic Terra Cotta Company's Abbochrome material for the frieze, panels and inserts of entrances, pier caps, and coping of the Coliseum on the State Fair grounds in Tulsa, Oklahoma.[20] Panels on the Coliseum were modeled to portray the character and purpose of the building—exhibiting livestock. To reduce the cost of shipping, terra-cotta was manufactured at various plants, such as the southern plant for Atlanta Terra Cotta Company in Georgia, which produced the material for the Coliseum.

Opposite top left. Charles Theater, 409 North Main Street, Charles City, Iowa, 1935–36, Wetherell & Harrison, architects.

Opposite top right. Midtown Theater (Metro Theater), 2626 Broadway, New York, New York, 1933, Boak & Paris, architects.

Opposite bottom left. Warehouse Market, 901 South Elgin Avenue, Tulsa, Oklahoma, 1929, B. Gaylord Noftsger, architect.

Opposite bottom right. Park Plaza Apartments, 1005 Jerome Avenue, Bronx, New York, 1928, Horace Ginsbern, architect.

Right. Gramercy Apartments, 235 East Twenty-second Street, New York, New York, 1928, George Blum & Edward Blum, architects.

MOSAIC

Transparent glass mosaic as art deco ornament was influenced by an earlier artist, Louis Comfort Tiffany, who created stunning effects by varying tone and color, achieved by gradiated bands of color or using iridescent material.[21] Various artists during the modernistic era exploited this medium, the palette for which could contain more than five hundred colors, in addition to metallics, but perhaps none so adroitly as Hildreth Meiere. Meiere's mosaics at the Nebraska State Capitol were the subject of several articles, including one written by Eugene Clute for *Architectural Forum*.[22] In addition to being editor of *The Metal Arts*, Clute contributed to other miscellaneous architecture and design journals. These articles were often devoted to a specific material or medium and its use in modernistic design.[23] A major commission for Hildreth Meiere in New York City was the Irving Trust Company lobby at One Wall Street, designed by Ralph Walker of Voorhees, Gmelin & Walker. Clute wrote several articles analyzing the decorative program of the Irving Trust Company building.[24] Describing Meiere's process of working on the lobby, Clute explained, "During the development of the design, Hildreth Meiere acted as a consultant for color and the scale of the decoration. Miss Meiere hung up in her studio a color scale representing the gradations from the darkest red at the dado [of Deerco rouge marble] to the orange of the ceiling and painted in upon the drawings of the motives the coloring in the same upward gradation. A portion of the large motive was enlarged photographically and color was applied to it. She also made various other color studies upon drawings and models."[25] Ravenna Mosaics executed this commission, and to produce the murals, artisans affixed tesserae to full-size working drawings and laid the paper on the wall with the tiles facing a cement bond.[26] After it was firm, the paper was washed away, then the tiles were grouted with dark blue on the walls and black grout on the ceiling.[27] An innovative aspect of the lobby mosaic was the incorporation of metal grilles and lighting fixtures designed by Walter Kantack, a major designer of the period. These lighting fixtures were integrated into the mosaics.[28]

Below. Irving Trust Company, One Wall Street, New York, New York, 1932. Voorhees, Gmelin & Walker, architects. Varying metallic shades were produced using gold alloyed with silver, copper, or other metals. The Ravenna mosaic technique is distinguished by a greater freedom and variety of handling the materials resulting from tesserae of different sizes.

Opposite. Irving Trust Company. Selected to entice the public, warm red and orange mosaics (created by Hildreth Meiere) cover the lobby walls. The brecciated Deerco rouge marble is reflected in the approximate size of the tesserae used on the lower section of the mosaic walls.

MAIN LOBBY
AND
INFORMATION DESK
STRAIGHT AHEAD

The architects, artists, craftsmen, and designers of the 1920s and 1930s used new or revived techniques for these materials to create the modernistic style. Among the many artists who contributed to the style's development, a few, having distinct styles and techniques, had greater impact, including artist Edgar Miller. Miller and Sol Kogen (who had attended the Chicago Art Institute with Miller but was essentially the real estate developer) bought rundown Victorian houses in Chicago and rebuilt them in an eclectic modernistic manner, frequently using recycled materials they scavenged. Miller was the architect and designer, working in numerous media: wood, stained glass, and mosaic collages of tiles, glass, and brick. Years later, when the restoration artist Robert Horn asked him what these complexes were about, Miller responded, "Fun. Having fun."[29]

Miller, like many artists of the period, was strongly influenced by Native American culture; his personal exposure came from his Idaho childhood. When he was thirteen, his father took him into the Australian bush for two years, after which he returned to Chicago to study with George Bellows at the Art Institute of Chicago. Miller then apprenticed for four years with Alfonso Ianelli.[30] He was responsible for the ornament in the State Capitol Building in Bismarck, North Dakota; the Memorial Hall window was featured in *The Architectural Forum* (February 1935) with the following copy: "Miller proceeds boldly in lead and glass, for instance, without benefit of cartoon, matching colors, and cutting forms in accordance with a vivid and compelling inner sight."[31] Among other commissions, Miller produced stained glass for the windows at Portage Junior High School in Chicago, which illustrate La Salle's explorations; the Marco Polo Room in the Waldorf-Astoria; and the high-relief sculptural ornament for Northwestern University's Technological Center at Evanston, which symbolizes earth, water, air, and fire.[32]

Above. Ahwahnee Hotel, Yosemite Village, California, 1927. Gilbert Stanley Underwood, architect; Jeannette D. Spencer, stained glass. Stenciled molding, carved wooden screen, lobby.

Although individual architects and artists had distinctive styles, decoration companies had even broader opportunities to influence modernistic style. Two major firms, Rambusch Decorating Company and Anthony B. Heinsbergen, executed various commissions ranging from metalwork to stained glass in every region of the United States. They employed sculptors, painters, and woodworkers. Rambusch engaged in the invention, design, and fabrication of church lighting fixtures; it patented a recessed downlight in 1934.[33] Architects Bley & Lyman, Dietel & Wade, Henry V. Murphy, and Cross & Cross worked with Rambusch; the company's designers, Knud Laub for instance, developed the architect's concepts into scale drawings. Even companies such as American Seating employed artists such as Alois Lang, who produced woodwork for Buffalo City Hall.[34]

Opposite. Ahwahnee Hotel. Massive furniture was created specifically for the Great Lounge.

Alois Lang, a skilled woodworker, produced carved wood doors and pews for the Shrine of the Little Flower in Detroit. He was born in Oberammergau, Germany, where he trained in wood carving, and came to the United States

Top left. Eastern Columbia Outfitters, 849 South Broadway, Los Angeles, California, 1929, Claude Beelman, architect.

Top right. Garfield Building, 408 West Eighth Street, Los Angeles, California, 1930, Claude Beelman, architect.

Above. I. Magnin, 2001–11 Broadway, Oakland, California, 1931, Weeks & Day, architects.

Opposite. Sunset Tower, 18358 Sunset Boulevard, Los Angeles, California, 1929, Leland A. Bryant, architect.

at age nineteen. He worked in Boston prior to moving to Manitowoc, Wisconsin, where he worked for the church division of the American Seating Company.[35] He often made preliminary studies in clay. Lang preferred working with oak and softer limewood, and used the fumes of ammonia to color the woods.[36] His work appears in Girard College Chapel, Philadelphia; Christ Church, Boston; Temple Emanu-El, New York; First Unitarian Church, Buffalo; and Christ Church at Cranbrook, Royal Oaks, Michigan.

Ultimately, American deco was a dominant style in the 1920s and 1930s, partially as a result of the collaborative efforts of men and women like Miller, Lang, and Meiere, in addition to the intense creative environment of design firms committed to a modern aesthetic. Excited by new materials and techniques, these artists expanded the boundaries of their fields' technologies; attuned to the American mystique, they were deeply committed to a decorative program which emerged, they believed, from its native soil. The exteriors and interiors in this book provide access to the artists and architects who created a distinctive American art deco style, as well as a glimpse of the lifestyle and aesthetics of a vibrant period. Although photographic documents are a form of historic preservation, they are not a substitute for conservation of these buildings' architectural integrity. It is hoped that we will be inspired to prevent further losses or degradation of buildings which may not yet be designated landmarks, and vigilantly protect those which are designated as such.

THE NEW YORK HOSPITAL

THE NORTHEAST

A major influence affecting urban density in northeastern cities in the early part of the twentieth century was the enormous influx of immigrants, who supplied labor for an expanding industrial-based economy. By 1930, 73.3 percent of the nearly eight million New York City residents were first- or second-generation immigrants.[1] These millions of immigrants—Italians, Swedes, Irish, Polish, Chinese, and Germans, among innumerable others—created a "New World Symphony" of cultures.[2] Ethnicity was identity in densely populated regions, which could seem overwhelmingly anonymous, and architects often alluded to specific cultural styles in the construction of new buildings, especially churches. The 1931 First Swedish Baptist Church in Manhattan, designed by Martin C. Hedmark, is a perfect example of ethnic influence in art deco architecture.

In addition to ecclesiastical buildings, banks, hotels, office towers, manufacturing lofts, apartment buildings, department stores, and civic buildings were constructed in rapid succession in the Northeast before the 1929 crash on Wall Street, and a large proportion of these were built in the modernistic style. Travel for pleasure and business had increased because of the expansion of modes and speed of transportation. One could now travel by plane, train, or automobile. Numerous hotels were constructed in urban regions of the Northeast to accommodate this trend. One of the major hotels built in New York City was Leonard Schultz & S. Fullerton Weaver's Waldorf-Astoria Hotel. Schultz & Weaver's associates were John F. Bacon, William Sunderland, E. V. Meroni, and Lloyd Morgan. Built for travelers and permanent residents, the hotel was lavish and included a magnificent three-story ballroom. The murals in the Grand Foyer are by Louis Rigal, who also designed the elevator doors.

New York Cornell Hospital, York Avenue between
East Sixty-eighth and East Seventy-first Streets to FDR Drive,
1933, Coolidge, Shepley, Bulfinch & Abbott, architects.

WORLD FOR MA
Y CONTAIN·IS
OMPASSED BY
BUDGET CUTS ARE
CING THE LIBRARY
REDUCE HOURS

Companies and manufacturers of new consumer products needed office towers and manufacturing space. Government services expanded; post offices, recreation facilities, and administrative offices were built to serve an increasing population. Economic prosperity caused intense real estate speculation in every region of the United States, not only the Northeast. "There is scarcely a city which does not show a bright new cluster of skyscrapers at its center," F. L. Allen wrote in 1931. "The tower building mania has reached its climax in New York—since towers in the metropolis are a potent advertisement—and particularly in the Grand Central District."[3]

Pinnacle, Empire State Building, New York, New York, 1931, Shreve, Lamb & Harmon, architects.

Urban density had led to one of the great American architectural innovations, the skyscraper. The form and technology of the skyscraper developed from skeletal construction utilizing a "curtain wall," instead of the historical load-bearing wall.[4] The decrease in weight as a result of the airy skeleton permitted the evolution of taller and taller buildings, especially as steel replaced cast iron and elevators began to be incorporated. Gradually, from the 1890s on, rational construction—where function determined form—supplanted stylistically motivated architecture. A new American cityscape was being created. In 1916 New York City became the first municipality to control height and density of the built environment through zoning regulations.[5] Complicated formulas limited building height for the street line and mandated that the buildings be set back at various levels to prevent claustrophobic congestion and canyons of shadow with little sunlight or air circulation. "Setbacks" resulted in stepped pyramidal profiles or a stepped base with a tall shaft or slab for the upper floors. Ely Jacques Kahn's Bricken Casino, located in New York City's garment district, exemplifies this stepped massing. The Empire State Building, the Newsweek Building (444 Madison Avenue, designed in 1931 by Kohn, Vitola & Knight), the 1933 New York Hospital-Cornell Medical Center (designed by Coolidge, Shepley, Bulfinch & Abbott), the Chrysler Building in midtown, and the Cities Service Building on Wall Street all contributed to Manhattan's distinctive skyline.

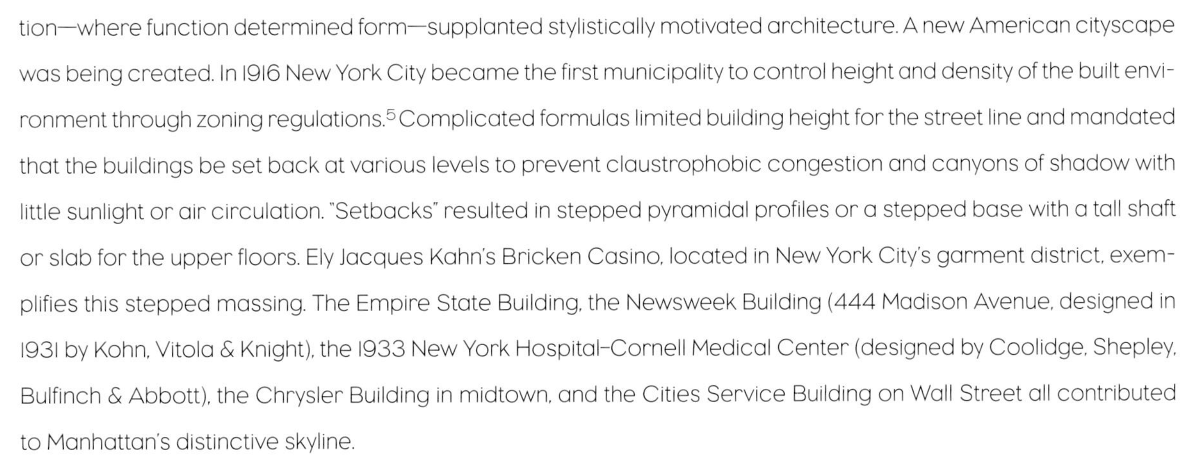

Due to its extreme height, the form of a skyscraper was often undiscernible to the pedestrian. Consequently, maquettes and images of a skyscraper's full elevation were often included in each building's decorative program, accessible at pedestrian level.[6] When the Fuller Construction Company built their corporate headquarters at Fifty-seventh Street and Madison Avenue, there was not only a pediment in the shape of a stylized urban skyline above the entrance (sculpted by Elie Nadelman), but the lobby floor incorporated roundels illustrating the Fuller Building, and earlier Fuller projects, including the 1903 Flatiron Building. Located on a narrow street in the Financial District, the Cities Service Building provides pedestrians with impressions of the building's form via Indiana limestone models of the skyscraper flanking each of the two main entrances.

Joseph H. Freedlander and Max Hausle designed the 1934 Bronx County Courthouse. *Progress*, the sculpture by Adolph A. Weinman which flanks the east entrance, depicts a muscular Moses holding a maquette of the building (although a more attenuated form than the actual structure) in place of the traditional tablets containing the Ten Commandments. *Progress* is a reflection of how religion had become inextricably incorporated into marketing real estate during the fervor of the 1920s. One of the largest property developers, Fred F. French, exhorted his salesmen

Opposite. Brooklyn Public Library, Grand Army Plaza, Brooklyn, New York, 1941, Githens & Keally, architects; C. Paul Jennewein, gilded sculptural reliefs.

to read Matthew 7:7, "by the Greatest Human Nature Expert who ever lived."[7] French reminded his salesmen that the greatest commandment was "Love Thy Neighbor as Thyself," and that as a result of this biblical injunction, the salesmen had "immeasurably strengthened their own characters and power, so that during this year they will serve our stockholders at a lower commission rate, and yet each one earn more money for himself than in nineteen hundred twenty-five."[8] The Metropolitan Casualty Insurance Company issued a pamphlet in the 1920s entitled "Moses, Persuader of Men," announcing that "Moses was one of the greatest salesmen and real-estate promoters that ever lived."[9]

For urban dwellers burdened by the stress of modern life, religious observances were perceived as an attempt to "cope with the too-bigness of life."[10] However, as the pace of living increased during the 1920s and 1930s, traditional practices of religion were eroded. Places of worship continued to be integral to urban lives, but often by providing centers for social and secular activities. The intensity and competitive spirit of the period is exemplified by the construction of St. John the Divine in Manhattan, intended to be the world's largest cathedral (construction has been almost continuous during the past century) and redesigned in the 1920s to reflect the Gothic modernism of Ralph Adams Cram. By the 1930s the Roman Catholic Church was constructing numerous churches in Brooklyn and Queens. Each ethnic group (and within these there were subgroups based on region or villages) had preferred saints, a contributing factor to increased ecclesiastical construction.[11] The Italian city of Siena revered St. Catherine, and immigrants from this region built churches in the New World dedicated to her. The National Shrine of St. Bernadette in Brooklyn was dedicated to the patron saint of sailors. An order founded in 1909, the Sisters of Saints Cyril and Methodius in Danville, Pennsylvania, built an academy to educate children of Slovak immigrants.

Opposite. Film Center, 630 Ninth Avenue, New York, New York, 1929, Buchman & Kahn, architects.

Every city in the Northeast was experiencing a similar phenomenon. Conrad Schmitt Studios, located in New York, produced such an abundance of work for churches that their advertisement in the periodical *Ecclesiastical Arts* referred to themselves as "Ecclesiologists."[12] Henry McGill's Church of the Most Precious Blood in Queens was an influential commission, published in numerous professional journals at the time to promote ecclesiastical modernism.[13] Henry Dagit & Sons designed the Crypt of St. Callistus Church in Philadelphia. A competition for the Girard College Chapel in Philadelphia culminated in the selection of architects Walter H. Thomas and Sydney E. Martin. Indicating the religious zeitgeist, Stephen Girard required that the chapel convey a distinct religious and moral impression yet avoid identification with any particular sect. The design selected was much more conservative than that submitted by Sternfeld, Zantzinger, Borie and Medary, Associated Architects, which was less classical and distinctly modernistic, with a ziggurat pinnacle.

The Metropolitan Building, 117 North Fifteenth Street, Philadelphia, Pennsylvania, 1926, Louis Jallade, architect. A French architect, Jallade designed the twenty-six story twin towered structure, one of the earliest art deco buildings in the city, encrusting the pinnacles and parapets with polychrome terra cotta.

Public building and urban infrastructure construction increased dramatically after World War I, and this trend continued after the stock market crash of 1929, as the federal government allocated millions of dollars for construction to stimulate the economy. For example, the New York City Department of Health, designed by Charles B. Meyers, was built on Worth Street in 1935. Courthouses and civic buildings pro-

Westchester County Center, 148 Martine Avenue, White Plains, New York, 1929, Walker & Gillette, architects, drawing by Earl Purdy.

Opposite. Waldorf-Astoria, 301 Park Avenue, New York, New York, 1931, Schultz & Weaver, architects; RCA Victor Building (GE), 570 Lexington Avenue, New York, New York, 1931, Cross & Cross, architects.

liferated. Walker & Gillette's 1929 Westchester County Center in White Plains, New York, displays the firm's signature form, the pier terminating in a flowing sconce. Funding for federal projects included resources to employ painters, sculptors, and other artists during the Depression, so that public buildings continued to be built and decorated in the modernistic mode, although the use of ornament declined and was virtually eliminated by World War II.

Formal abstraction in architectural details and design preceded the rise of nonrepresentational art. Architects were using geometrical ornament on industrial buildings in Chicago and New York City by 1900, partially influenced by architect and theorist Claude L. Bragdon. Bragdon was regarded by eminent architectural critic Lewis Mumford

Claude Bragdon, illustration for the application of geometric motifs, *Architectural Record*, 1927.

as one of the most influential theorists of the early twentieth century. Subscribing to the Theosophist, or transcendental, movement, Bragdon evolved a theory of geometric ornament as a manifestation of spiritual modernism. He considered this type of ornament to be the perfect expression of quantum physics and the transcendental experience.[14] The type of ornament he proposed was often utilized in art deco. Bragdon's discourses, frequently contributed to architectural journals, provided architects with a theory of applied decoration that "promotes the order which pervades the universe."[15] Claiming that even democracy was a "condition of consciousness" as well as a state of the soul, he composed essays on such disparate topics as "Harnessing the Rainbow" and "The World Order" in *Architecture and Democracy.* Democracy in this context referred to the process of creativity residing in individuals rather than any collective.[16] Finally, having spent time in Frank Lloyd Wright's atelier, Bragdon provided a major link between the Chicago School and the Eastern architectural establishment.

Bragdon's theories did not seem esoteric in a cultural milieu in which modernism was a moral issue. By 1930, Bragdon was considered an authority of architectural theory and was frequently quoted by architecture critics such as Sheldon Cheney. Architects as influential as Ralph Walker of Voorhees, Gmelin & Walker would state: "The new architecture will not be a thing of slab-sided cubes or spheres, built up of plane and solid geometry in which there is no element of time . . . but will have an infinite variety of complex forms and an intricate meaning that will be comprehensible to minds that are able to project thought beyond infinity."[17]

Modernity's "moral mandate" became popular in the United States after the 1902 publication of Thorstein Veblen's *Theory of the Leisure Class.* Delineating his theory of conspicuous consumption, Veblen, a brilliant economist, contrasted the excessively ornamental composite architectural styles (derivative of every historical period) of residential buildings with industrial buildings which, he explained, were clearly and simply expressive of purpose. Veblen found such expressiveness aesthetically appealing. "The endless variety of fronts presented by the better class of tenements and apartment houses in our cities is an endless variety of architectural distress and of suggestions of expensive discomfort," he wrote. "Considered as objects of beauty, the dead walls of the sides and back of these structures, left untouched by the hands of the artist, are commonly the best feature of the building."[18] These novel theories certainly contributed to the promotion of modernism in the early twentieth century.

Another early proponent of geometric ornament was the New Yorker Ely Jacques Kahn. By 1928 Kahn, a major architect and designer, had developed a distinctive style—he used plastic surfaces to express his modernism, such as projecting brick headers to create patterned shadows. Kahn was intrigued with the idea of exploring spatial and decorative issues on a pragmatic rather than a spiritual level. He emphasized the concept of the curtain wall, "weaving" textured ornament on surfaces of buildings. Kahn's firm, Buchman & Kahn, was responsible for more than 250 buildings during the modernist decades, and Kahn designed numerous buildings in the Garment District (the Bricken Casino, 42–44 West Thirty-ninth Street, and 1400 Broadway are excellent examples) and skyscrapers on Wall Street and Fifth Avenue (including the Squibb Building, unfortunately altered), as well as elsewhere in the city. The foyer and lobby of the Film Center are brilliant expressions of Kahn's secessionist tendencies. Kahn created a parody of film technology, with black marble bands encircling the elevator lobby to suggest rolls of unprocessed film and pink marble sprockets (aligning the film in a camera) projecting from the walls at the edges. Red enameled bronze dots refer to those affixed to large format camera lenses.[19]

The impact of photography was a great influence on the abstraction found in modernistic design. "Black and white images, especially of buildings, contained an essentially abstract message . . . utilitarian brick structures in harsh sunlight could transform three-dimensional reality into jazzy geometrical compositions of strong squares . . . [rectangles] and triangles."[20] Popular culture, science, and technology also affected motifs. The architects of the 1931 RCA Building (later owned by GE) used electromagnetic-wave imagery, zigzags, as a primary motif. The "giants of Wall Street" on City Bank Farmers Trust Building alternately scowl and smile across the façade, exhibiting popular culture's conflicted perception of financial instruments.

By 1928 *The Architectural Record,* published in New York City, had entirely revamped its design and contents to reflect the dominant paradigm, modernism, and the associated decline of historicism and composite styles. Numerous skyscrapers, warehouses, manufacturing lofts, apartments, and hotels were finished that year, and the ground was broken for many more. Slabs and towers, attenuated pyramids, and innovative pinnacles began to transform every city in the Northeast region into what immigrants had imagined the New World to be—a symbol of all that was modern, of the achievements of science, technology, and freedom.

RCA Victor Building (General Electric), 570 Lexington Avenue, New York, New York, 1931, Cross & Cross, architects, is a Gothicized art deco skyscraper with an imaginative polychrome and gold terra-cotta pinnacle. The vertical zigzags symbolize electromagnetic waves and radio communications.

FRED F. FRENCH BUILDING

551 Fifth Avenue, New York, New York, 1927. H. Douglas Ives (in-house architect for the French Company, a large developer) with John Sloan of Sloan & Robertson, architects.

2

3

The French Building is a thirty-eight-story skyscraper, one of the first to have a flat roof.

4

1. Detail of terra-cotta griffins.

2. Detail of upper floors with limestone coping and terra-cotta frieze. The beehive motif is symbolic of thrift and industry; the rising sun symbolizes progress, flanked by winged griffins representing integrity and vigilance.

3. Setback.

4. Detail of bronze lintel above Fifth Avenue Entrance.

5. A general view reveals the shallow setbacks and how the complex solution of imposed zoning regulations affected the form.

1

5

6

6. Elevator bank with inlaid brass marble pier; the ceilings are stenciled.

7. A sumptuous shopping arcade was built as an advertisement for the property developer, signifying the company's commitment to the civic spirit.

47

TUNNEL
TO E 46 ST
LEFT LANE
ONLY
8'-11"
CLEARANCE
FedEx
LANES FLOOR COVERING
TWO
FedEx

TWO PARK AVENUE

New York, New York, 1927, Ely Jacques Kahn (Buchman & Kahn), architect; Leon V. Solon, color consultant.

2

3

Two Park Avenue, a reinforced-concrete building clad with buff brick and brilliant polychrome terra-cotta cornices, coping, and spandrels, illustrated in *Architectural Record,* April 1928, and *Architecture and Building,* May 1928. Seward National Bank was originally the major ground-floor tenant. Hildreth Meiere often worked with Ely Jacques Kahn and may have produced the mosaics for the vestibule.

1. General view with the Empire State Building in the background.

2. Setbacks are delineated by polychrome terra-cotta coping.

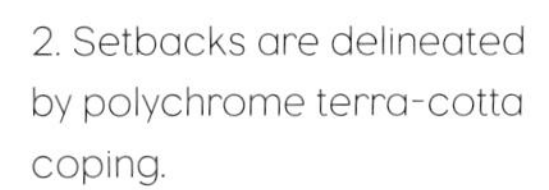

3. Elevator doors were executed by the Art Metal Construction Company and illustrated in *The Metal Arts,* January 1929.

4. Kahn and Leon V. Solon's use of color was scrutinized by professional journals; *The Architectural Record,* December 1927, and *The Architectural Forum,* September 1929, illustrated the building. Kahn, one of the most prolific architects working in the modernistic idiom, treated the surface as a textile, using terra-cotta surface textures horizontally to contrast with the warp, or vertical elements of the building. Federal Terra Cotta Company supplied the material.

5. The metalwork was executed by the Art Metal Construction Company.

6. Lobby mailbox.

4

5

6

1

GEORGE A. FULLER COMPANY BUILDING

41 East Fifty-seventh Street, New York, New York, 1929, Walker & Gillette, architects.

1

2

The forty-story skyscraper, was illustrated in *The Architectural Forum*, August 1931, and built by the Fuller Construction Company. In 1932, W. Parker Chase listed it fortieth of New York City's one hundred tallest skyscrapers.

1. Bronze light fixture, with highlights in gold finish, above the Fifty-seventh Street entrance.

2. The stylized pediment representing the New York City skyline above the Fifty-seventh Street entrance of the Fuller Building is constructed from cast concrete; the sculpture is by Elie Nadelman.

3. Lobby with a dado of Belgian black marble; marble mosaic rondels on the floor illustrate exceptional buildings erected by the Fuller Company.

4. Ziggurat pinnacle is clad in polished black granite. The Fuller Building was illustrated in *The Architectural Forum*, August 1931.

3

4

לא תרצח
לא תנאף
אנכי יהוה
אלהיך
לא תעשה
לך פסל

TEMPLE EMANU-EL

840 Fifth Avenue, New York, New York, 1929, Robert D. Kohn, Charles Butler, Clarence Stein, Mayers, Murray & Phillip, architects.

Temple Emanu-El replaced an earlier temple for the congregation. Oscar B. Bach designed and executed the forged iron torchères for the temple's narthex, which has a walnut-paneled ceiling. The narthex torchères were illustrated in *The Metal Arts,* November 1929. Except for the ornamental arch with Hildreth Meiere's mosaic, the walls of the main sanctuary are unornamented and clad in Acoustolith, a terra-cotta tile product supplied by Cuastavino and developed by Meiere in collaboration with Bertram Goodhue for its acoustical properties.

1. The modernistic Chapel was designed by Clarence Stein. Metal artist Oscar B. Bach designed and executed the Ark. The steel frame was designed to accommodate doors removed from the previous temple's Ark. The doors are cast bronze with ornament in low relief. Each door is a single casting and adapted by Bach by enriching the original doors with new ornamental motifs in copper repoussé illuminated with vitreous enamel in brilliant colors and gold. The Ark was illustrated in *The Metal Arts,* July 1929. Stained glass in the Chapel was made by d'Ascenzo Studios of Philadelphia. Chapel domes are supported by pink Westerly granite columns; side walls are supported by columns of Breche Oriental marble. Mosaics were produced by Otto Heinigke.

2

2. In the main sanctuary, the doors of the Ark, which contains the Torah, are bronze in a pierced overall design and slide on tracks to open. These, the menorahs, and the Perpetual Light were executed by Edward F. Caldwell & Company. Fine mosaics by Meiere cover the walls of the Bema. Columns flanking the Ark are French Benou Jaume marble. The pierced bronze screen was produced by Eli Berman & Company. W. K. Hase Decorators, Inc., executed painted decoration.

3

4

5

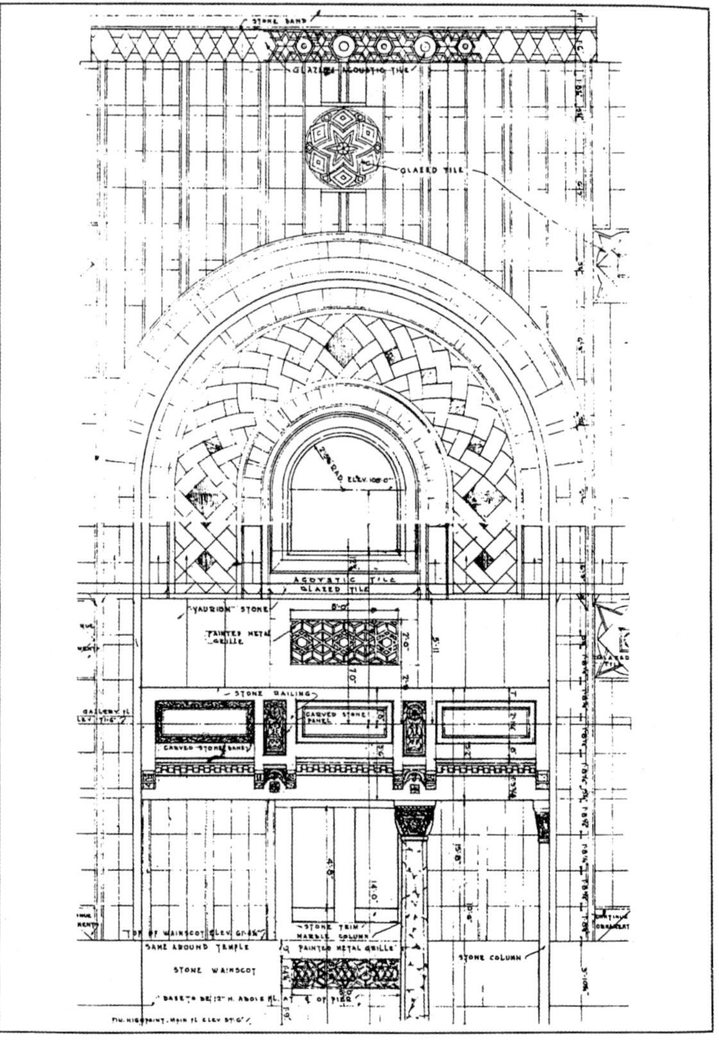
STONE BAND
GLAZED ACOUSTIC TILE
GLAZED TILE
ACOUSTIC TILE
GLAZED TILE
"YAURION" STONE
PAINTED METAL GRILLE
STONE RAILING
CARVED STONE PANEL
CARVED STONE BAND
TOP OF WAINSCOT ELEV. 61-6½"
SAME AROUND TEMPLE
STONE WAINSCOT
STONE TRIM
MARBLE COLUMN
PAINTED METAL GRILLE
STONE COLUMN

6

3. Bronze transom grilles were produced by the General Bronze Corporation.

4. Lighting fixtures in the halls were produced by Black and Boyd Manufacturing Company. Stair balusters are hand-forged white metal and iron, made by Frank & Pilny, Inc.

5. Tower pinnacle.

6. Drawing, detail of side walls and gallery, *Architectural Forum*, February 1930.

7. Enameled metal ornamental details of the Ark in the Chapel were inserted at points in the rails and stiles and in the centers of the large circular motifs in the panels, replacing original ornament which was removed to accommodate Bach's modernistic work.

CHRYSLER BUILDING

405 Lexington Avenue, New York, New York, 1930, William Van Alen, architect.

The Chrysler Building was published in *American Architect,* September 1930. A radiating zigzag motif on the pinnacle is a modernistic allusion to the Statue of Liberty's crown, created from sheet metal and executed by Benjamin Riesner, Inc. Krupp's formula steel, a material with exceptional strength and high resistance to corrosion, was produced by Crucible Steel Company. Metalwork for the lobby and stairwells was illustrated in *The Metal Arts,* July/August 1930.

1. The polychrome terra-cotta pinnacle of the Townhouse Apartment Building appears in the foreground, against the Chrysler's modernistic latticed steel terminus, termed a vertex. One hundred and eighty feet high, 8 feet 7 inches at the base, the vertex was manufactured by Post & McCord in three segments that were assembled in the fire tower to conceal its presence from the competing Cities Service Building being erected by Clinton & Russell with Holton & George.

2. Steel for the Chrysler Building was nickel chromium, KA-2 Steel, Krupp's formula, produced by Crucible Steel Company, Central Alloy, and several others. The pinnacle's spandrels were cast by Rembrandt Studios, finished by sandblasting, and highlighted with a medium polish.

3. Stainless-steel pineapples emphasize the setback.

4. Steel radiator-cap gargoyles and patterned brick forming a wheel motif.

2

3

4

5

Lexington Avenue Entrance

Plan

Elevation

Section

6

5. Lexington Avenue entrance detail, *American Architect*, September 1930.

6. Morocco rouge flammé marble streamed with white and other colors clads the interior walls of the lobby. The ceiling mural, *Energy, Result, Workmanship and Transportation*, was painted by Edward Trumbull. Lighting engineer H. S. Arnold conceived of indirect-lighting sources via the octagonal pillars in the grand foyer, which have V-shaped recesses and are lined with amber onyx in vertical reflector troughs.

7. Light sources over the elevator lobbies utilize honed Mexican onyx, and reflectors in the steel casing. Lighting fixtures were produced by the Frink Corporation. The lobby floor is Sienna travertine.

8. Elevator door detail of inlaid woods executed by the Tyler Company and illustrated in *The Metal Arts*, May 1930.

7

CITIES SERVICE BUILDING

(AIG) 70 Pine Street, New York, New York, 1932, Clinton & Russell and Holton & George, architects.

2

3

4

The Cities Service Building competed with the Chrysler Building to be the tallest structure in New York City.

For efficiency, double elevator cabs delivered passengers to two floors simulataneously.

1. Indiana limestone maquettes of the building flank entrances on north and south elevations.

2. Rendering courtesy of the Landmark Society of Western New York.

3. Lobby detail of aluminum stair rails.

4. Interior of lobby.

CHURCH OF THE MOST PRECIOUS BLOOD

32-30 Thirty-seventh Street, Long Island City, New York, 1932, Henry J. McGill, architect.

The church was illustrated in *American Architect*, December 1932, and *Liturgical Arts*, October 1932. Exterior masonry consists of seam-face granite mixed with 10 percent split face. The other walls are faced with wire-cut brick.

1. The pierced aluminum crown of the tower is satin-finished. The piercing technique came into vogue as the result of new technology, such as oxyacetylene, providing metal artists greater freedom to cut patterns into metal. McGill used this technique in the Church of the Most Precious Blood as a metaphor for the nails by which Jesus was hung from the Cross.

2. The Cross above the altar is St. Victor rose marble inlaid with Numidian red marble; ruby glass and aluminum grille strip light fixtures flank the Cross and represent the Blood of Christ.

3. Stations of the Cross were painted by D. Dunbar Beck of the Conrad Schmitt Studios.

4. Elevation drawings of the principal façade reveal McGill's use of a cross motif. *American Architect*, December 1932.

5. Faience tiles are interspersed in the granite finish terra-cotta dado on the interior of the church. Grilles and other decorative metal are aluminum. The Blessed Virgin and St. Joseph were carved from Carrara marble by Hazel Clere.

2

3

4

5

ST. ANDREW AVELLINO CHURCH

157-01 Northern Boulevard, Queens, New York, 1940, Henry V. Murphy, architect, Herman Veit, contractor.

1

The church was built with reinforced concrete, limestone, and tapestry brick as the result of generous donations from the Ronzoni family.

1. General view.

2. A massive bronze medallion includes the Creek cross within a rondel of foliated patterns and peacocks, symbolic of the beauty of the Roman Catholic religion. Weighing two tons, the medallion is attached to black granite on the facade.

3. Shrine of the Sacred Passion; stained glass fabricated by Daprato Studio.

4. The altar is the ciborium type cut from St. Victor rose marble. The reredos is white bronze with antique gold rosettes.

2

3

4

S. LUCAS
S. MARCUS
IOANNES
CARITAS

BRONX COUNTY COURTHOUSE

851 Grand Concourse, Bronx, New York, 1931, Joseph H. Freedlander and Max Hausle, architects.

1

The Courthouse is a symmetrical block design, with an entrance on each elevation constructed of Indiana limestone. Compensating for the slight hill on which it is situated, Bronx County Courthouse is elevated by a rusticated granite podium. Sculptures on 161st Street are by George H. Snowden; the Walton Avenue sculptures are by Joseph Kiselewski.

1. South elevation. Edward F. Sanford was responsible for the 158th Street elevation sculptures, which flank the stairs to the entrance; *Triumph of Government* and *Genius of Administration* are carved from Georgia pink marble.

2. The friezes on the four elevations by Charles Keck are identical and describe the labor of man, agriculture, commerce, industry, religion, the arts, war, and enslavement.

3. Detail of Sanford's *Genius of Administration.*

4. Detail of east elevation and ornament at first setback.

2

3

4

6

7

8

5. Bronze transom and door grille on 158th Street elevation.

6. Detail of cast bronze transom grille inlaid with nickel.

7. *The Song of Achievement* and *Progress* appear on the Grand Concourse elevation, sculpted by Adolph A. Weinman.

8. General view of Bronx County Courthouse.

RYE PLAYLAND

Playground Parkway, Rye, New York, 1927, Walker & Gillette, architects.

2

3

4

Rye Playland was designed in a "logical" modern style to replace an earlier amusement park scattered on Rye Beach in Westchester County. Facilities include large bathhouses, an arcade, and a music tower with bandstand.

1. Amusement park buildings.

2. Pinnacle of music tower and bandstand.

3. Elevation of music tower and bandstand, illustrated in *The Architectural Record*, May 1928.

4. Detail of wood arcade near parking.

5. Boardwalk and bathhouses influenced by Mediterranean architecture.

1

5

NIAGARA MOHAWK POWER CORPORATION

300 Erie Boulevard West, Syracuse, New York, 1930, Bley & Lyman, architects.

1

2

The Niagara Mohawk Power Corporation building is a six-story buff brick-clad structure. Known for designing office buildings for public-service companies, Bley & Lyman's work was published in *The Architectural Record,* December 1932, illustrated by another building—the Niagara Hudson in Olean, New York.

1. *Spirit of Light* sculpture.

2. Detail of transom grille and marquee above entrance.

3. General view.

NIAGARA MOHAWK

BUFFALO CITY HALL

65 Niagara Square, Buffalo, New York, 1929–31, George J. Dietel & John J. Wade, Sullivan Jones, architects.

Buffalo City Hall was built to consolidate city offices formerly dispersed among numerous buildings. It was the largest (thirty stories), and most opulent city hall built at the time, costing $6,816,914.

1. Transom panels over each doorway at the main entrance represent American pioneers. Kasota limestone was used for facing and sculptures; granite for the elongated octagonal base was quarried in Amherst and Briar Hill, Ohio.

2. Polychrome terra-cotta tiles create stylized Native American motifs on the upper levels and pinnacle of the City Hall.

1

2

3

4

5

6

7

3. Detail of limestone ornament.

4. The City Council Chamber located at the setback thirteenth floor is partially illuminated by daylight. Stylized Native American motifs inspired the stenciled ceiling framed by a brass cornice band with gold leaf. Original furnishings accommodate 383 persons.

5. Albert T. Stewart sculpted the frieze above the entrance portico portraying the social history of Buffalo.

6. Bryant Baker's sculpture of President Millard Fillmore, who was from Buffalo.

7. The City Council Chamber's stained glass ceiling relies on prisms to diffuse light.

8. City Council Chamber stained glass ceiling and windows.

8

THE SISTERS OF SAINTS CYRIL AND METHODIUS SLOVAK GIRLS ACADEMY

(The Sisters of Saints Cyril and Methodius) 580 Railroad Street, Danville, Pennsylvania, 1933, Harry Sternfeld & B. E. Starr; Henry Dagit & Sons, architects.

1

2

The Basilica, Holy Family Convent, was published in *Architecture,* July 1932, and *Liturgical Arts,* October 1940, and has an imposing campanile composed of four buttresses of proportions which diminish with height and pierced tracery.

1. General view of the academy, which is now defunct, although the convent remains. The tower symbolizes the grace and beauty of pure scholarship.

2. Exterior with cast stone details produced by Formigli & Son.

3. Detail of bronze alter rail. Tennessee marble covers the floor.

4. Interior of Basilica faced with Italian travertine.

3

4

NIAT REGNUM
387
31
1.4
A
Ω

BERKS COUNTY COURTHOUSE

633 Court Street, Reading, Pennsylvania, 1931. William H. Dechant & Sons, M. B. Dechant, architect; F. H. Dechant, engineer.

2

3

The rather lavish courthouse was built to reflect Reading's position in the twentieth century. The city had a major railroad line and heavy industry which consisted of over 700 factories that produced 300 types of products

1. Writing desk in lobby.

2. Bronze eagles and transom grille on east elevation entrance. Permutations of the American eagle were endless and so rampant in civic construction that *Architecture*, May 1933, featured a portfolio of the eagle in architectural sculpture.

3. Elevator doors in lobby.

4. Indiana limestone gargoyles.

5. Detail of stenciled ceiling.

6. West entrance foyer.

4

5

6

UNITED STATES COURTHOUSE AND WILLIAM PENN ANNEX POST OFFICE

(Robert C. Nix Courthouse) 900 Market Street, Philadelphia, Pennsylvania, 1940, The Ballinger Company & Harry Sternfeld, architects.

1

2

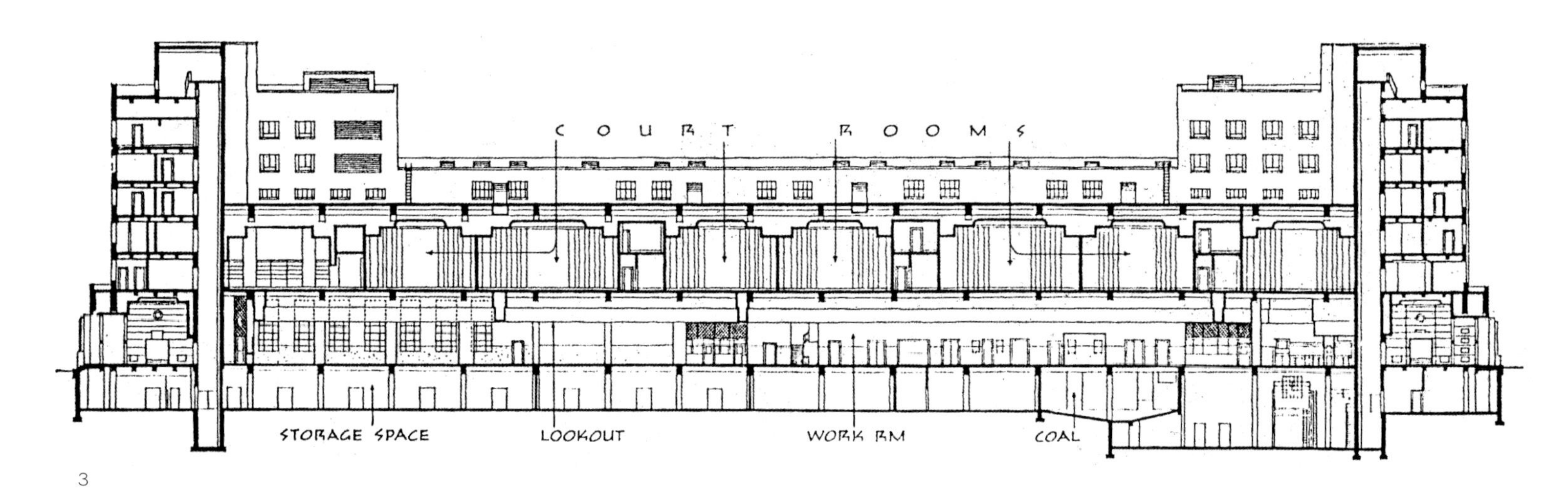

3

The Courthouse is a monolithic reinforced-concrete building that occupies an entire city block.

1. Large sculptural panels on the Chestnut Street entrances are the work of Donald De Lue of New York.

2. Sculpture flanking the Chestnut Street entrance.

3. Longitudinal section, *Pencil Points*, September 1941.

4. The limestone cladding is subtly enhanced by sculptures in granite on the Ninth Street entrance, by Edmond Amateis of Brewster, New York.

4

UNITED STATES POST OFFICE
WILLIAM PENN ANNEX
LETTERS
POST OFFICE

S & W
CAFETERIA
S&W BUILDING
SHOTZY'

THE SOUTH

The South has a colorful and complex history. Portions have belonged to the French and Spanish Crowns. Delicate wrought-iron work from French architecture and rope cable columns from the Spanish influenced art deco in this region. The verdant environment of the South and its climate provided inspiration for numerous motifs found in its regional art deco, which, in combination with the exoticism of Mediterranean and Spanish architecture, created memorable buildings. Dense everglades and treacherous shoals kept the region largely underpopulated until the advent of various industries in the early twentieth century, except for cities such as New Orleans, which had already developed as a major port, and Shreveport, experiencing an oil boom. Edward Neild, architect of the Maricopa County Building in Phoenix, Arizona, designed several outstanding examples of art deco in Shreveport.[1] The South also remained a conservative citadel, perpetuating the Greek revival style. Spanish Colonial and Mediterranean began to gain ascendancy as the styles of choice in Florida during the 1920s simply as a marketing ploy, the beguiling exoticism referring to the climate.[2] Even Kress stores in the region are less deco than classical or Spanish Colonial. In addition to the South's conservatism, the Depression had a devastating effect on the building-related industries. A survey of issues of *The Southern Architectural Review* (1936–37) and *Southern Architect and Building News* during the early 1930s reveals the paucity of new construction, compared to other regions in the United States. Construction supported by federal programs produced a new state prison for Georgia in 1937,[3] a post office building in High Point, North Carolina, designed by Everhart, Voorhees, Workman & Eckles, in 1934,[4] and the Allied Arts Building in Lynchburg, Virginia.[5]

S & W Cafeteria,
5258 Patton Avenue, Asheville,
North Carolina, 1927–28,
Douglas Ellington, architect.

S & W Cafeteria. Detail of metal marquee and polychrome terra cotta.

In contrast, in the early twentieth century, Florida was developing a robust tourist industry, and construction associated with land development there provided the impetus for economic prosperity. Henry B. Plant, on the west coast of Florida, and Henry M. Flagler, on the east coast, constructed railroads and lavish hotels at the turn of the century to create winter resorts which initially attracted the socially elite from the eastern seaboard, but later attracted the middle class as well. Tourism fueled real estate speculation; by 1925 there were approximately two thousand real estate offices and twenty-five thousand salesmen.[6] After the devastating hurricane in 1926, Miami rebuilt, but Miami Beach was developed later and the hotels built there tend toward the Moderne style—streamlined, with fewer embellishments and forms derived from ships and airplanes. A particularly regional characteristic of art deco in Miami Beach is the cantilevered form, providing shade to alleviate the tropical climate. Few of the hotels, however, have maintained their architectural and interior integrity, probably because of appropriation for military personnel during World War II. The National Hotel is an exception; the bar and its furnishings, as well as chairs and couches in the lobby, are original.

One of the first major residential developers in the 1920s was George Merrick, who created Coral Gables (named for the native pink limestone) near Miami by subdividing the grapefruit plantation he had inherited as part of his father's estate. Although it is primarily Spanish Mediterranean, he originally intended to build sixteen foreign-theme compounds. The Chinese village was designed with Henry Killam Murphy, who designed eight homes, influenced by Beijing houses of the Ming dynasty, which he had seen during his travels.[7] Coral Gables remains intact, a charming remnant of the boom years.

A unique architectural talent emerged in North Carolina during the 1920s. Douglas Ellington became one of the significant architects of the region, ultimately designing Greenbelt, Maryland, the earliest planned community constructed by the federal government. He studied architecture at Drexel Institute and the University of Pennsylvania under Paul P. Cret; in 1911 he was awarded the Paris Prize, which enabled him to study at the *École des Beaux-Arts* in Paris. Ellington was the first American ever to be awarded the Prix Rougevin, for decorative competitions at the school.[8] When World War I began, Ellington returned to the United States and, joining the navy, was assigned to a new division, the Camouflage Department. Ellington opened his own office in Philadelphia after the war and was awarded the commission to design the First Baptist Church in Asheville, North Carolina, where he moved in 1924 to supervise construction. An original architect, Ellington designed a church which was purely modernistic and attracted wide publicity, including coverage in the August 1930 edition of *The Architectural Record.* Ellington next obtained the commission to design Asheville City Hall.

While engaged in these and other commissions, Ellington was building his own house on Chunn's Cove with materials scavenged from the church (red Booker brick), Asheville City Hall (Georgia pink marble, buff brick), and the new high school building (Balfour Pink, a local granite, and Airedale brick).[9] He salvaged from other sources as well. The original building was a log cabin, chinked with stone and concrete, to which Ellington added a living room whose size was determined by that of logs from a schoolhouse being torn down. Some of the steps on the interior are curbing from the city of Asheville and Belgian block from the streets. The hardware on doors and windows was hand-forged by Daniel Boone, who had a forge in Burnside, North Carolina, and was a descendant of the iconic Daniel Boone. The woodwork, designed by Ellington and often utilizing a chevron motif, was produced by Hugh Brown, who had an antique and cabinet shop in Asheville.[10] Iron grilles on doors were made from material which is the precursor of rebar and was used in concrete work at the time. Boone made the fireplace andirons from brass fire-hose nozzles. Exterior brick, with various colors of enamel paint on the surfaces, came from a building being torn down which had a sign painted on it.[11] Guastavino provided tiles and engineering for the entrance arcade on City Hall, and Ellington incorporated tile remnants into his home as well. Ellington was known as a jackdaw, salvaging materials from any available source.[12] Other young architects and draftsmen provided labor, allowing him to limit costs related to construction and create the charming Chunn's Cove residence, built and landscaped to conform with the contours of the hill, surrounded by mountains.

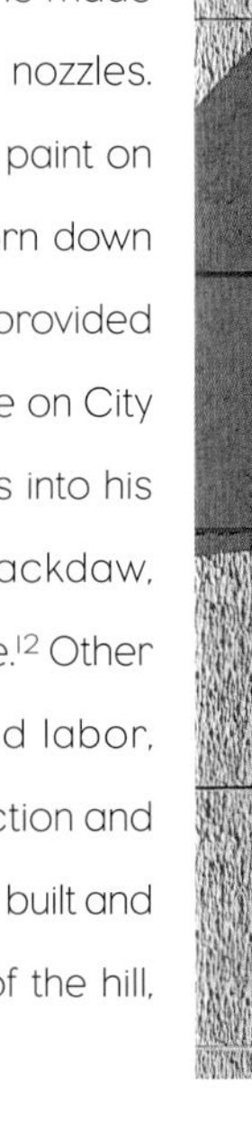

S & W Cafeteria. Detail.

Birmingham, Alabama, was booming in the 1920s—iron and nitrate plants were under construction. A ten-story skyscraper commissioned by the Jemison Company was built by a firm producing numerous residential and institutional projects, Warren, Knight & Davis. Eugene H. Knight apprenticed to gain his architectural knowledge; William T. Warren studied at Columbia University after obtaining an engineering degree from the Alabama Polytechnic Institute; and John E. Davis joined the firm in 1921.[13] After Warren, Knight, & Davis was engaged by Alabama Power and Light in 1924 to design a corporate office tower, a condition was imposed that the firm collaborate with APL's in-house architect, Sigmund Nesselroth of New York.[14] Prior to the Alabama Power and Light project, the firm was known for designs typical of the period, revival and composite styles, and it seems probable that Nesselroth's influence affected the modernistic direction of the skyscraper. Following this commission and one other modernistic skyscraper, the firm's work continued in its usual historic revival styles. Edward Sanford, a nationally recognized sculptor whose studio was in New York City, carved the pediment statues in situ. He also created the cast-bronze statue on the pinnacle.

Opposite. Douglas Ellington's Chunn's Cove residence, Asheville, North Carolina, 1929–35. Kitchen.

In Louisiana, Huey Pierce Long was actively lobbying to build a new capitol. A charismatic but conflicted individual who read law at Tulane University, Long was granted an exception to take the law exam early. Long had experienced hardship growing up as one of nine children, so he identified with the working poor.[15] He was elected governor on a platform of social justice, quoting William Jennings Bryan, "Every man a king." Long was viewed with ambivalence by the wealthy, and feared by others for his vindictive personality—he was known to build highways to bypass towns which had not voted for him. He was elected to the United States Senate in 1930. After funding was obtained to build a new capitol, he happened to attend the dedication of a building built by Seiferth, Weiss & Dreyfous. Mentioning to Leon Weiss that he was seeking an architect to design the new capitol, Weiss responded that their firm would gladly accept the commission, and work commenced the following day.[16] An extraordinary team of artists and craftsmen was assembled to build this modernistic capitol. Long insisted on only two parameters: it should be a skyscraper, and the ornamental program should revolve around the state's history. On September 8, 1935, Long was assassinated in the Memorial Hall at the capitol. A commemorative statue by Charles Keck in 1940 marks his grave in front of the capitol he built.[17]

The 1931 Kennedy-Warren Apartments, located in Washington, D.C., is an example of the apartment hotel, one of the results of the material feminist movement in the United States, which forged an acceptance of apartments as an appropriate residential form for the middle class.[18] The cooperative dining feature was often incorporated into this type of building, which offered not only dining services but housekeeping suites containing kitchenettes for those who desired to cook, daily maid services, a central lobby, and often libraries and other informal public spaces. Combining services offered by hotels and long-term leases, these dual-service buildings enabled one to set up housekeeping with a minimum of effort, especially useful as people streamed into the urban centers. The commercial aspect of these buildings

Left. Residence, Miami Beach, Florida.

TIONAL
THE NATIONAL

Above. Example of generic art deco concrete ornament, Miami Beach, Florida; colors are recent.

Opposite. National Hotel, 1677 Collins Avenue, Miami Beach, Florida, 1939, Roy F. France, architect. Lobby bar with original furniture.

led architects to apply modernistic design as a ploy to advertise the buildings' modern features and comforts.

Atlanta, Georgia, was another center where modernistic work was constructed. The 1929 Southern Bell Building, designed by Marye, Alger & Vinour, containing long-distance telephone equipment, had wonderful sculptural details, including a line repairman and an operator.[19] Unfortunately, as in virtually all telephone buildings surveyed in the United States, a loss of integrity has been occurring. The W. W. Orr Building, medical offices located in Atlanta, is a wonderful example of modernistic design, and has a high degree of integrity.

Beguiling examples of regional art deco are found in the South, and Louisiana's State Capitol Building is representative of the singular talent of architects and artists in this region. Architects such as Douglas Ellington were concerned with modernistic motifs that were influenced by the region, even to the extent of mediating the color of the buildings, which arose from the regional red earth (Asheville City Hall). If the economic prosperity of the 1920s had not been interrupted by the Depression, there would, no doubt, be numerous examples of art deco in the large cities of the South. As it was, small towns often had at least one example of modernistic architecture (usually a movie theater such as the Martin Theater in Talladega, Alabama, or the Tift Theater in Tifton, Georgia), indicating that, with greater economic resources, the region could have been a pivotal force in developing the modernistic style.

KENNEDY-WARREN APARTMENTS

3133 Connecticut Avenue, N.W., Washington, D.C., 1930–31, Joseph Younger, architect.

The Kennedy-Warren Apartments complex is an L-shaped reinforced concrete and buff brick structure on an Indiana limestone base. A majority of the ornament appears on the entrance pavilion.

1. Cast-aluminum marquee over the entrance pavilion to the apartments. The building was originally constructed as an apartment hotel and contains dining rooms, a library, a ballroom, and other public spaces.

2. General exterior view.

3. Carved limestone pediment over windows on the entrance pavilion.

4. Detail of central pavilion's pinnacle.

2

3

4

ASHEVILLE CITY BUILDING

70 Court Plaza, Asheville, North Carolina, 1926–27, Douglas D. Ellington, architect.

1

2

3

4

The Asheville City Building was built of steel framing in an equilateral form to express the democratic principal of equality. A transition from the lighter to the darker of the colors of brick, terra-cotta, and marble were selected to parallel the natural clay-pink shades of Asheville soil.

1. Rendering by Douglas Ellington, 1928, Asheville Art Museum; photograph by Paul Jeremias.

2. Loggia floors and wainscoting are honed-finish Georgia pink marble; walls are of variegated ocher tiles with a border of pink and black.

3. Prismatic bronze and opalescent glass torchères flank the entrance.

4. The interior of the City Council Chambers contains murals by Clifford Addams; topics of the murals were selected by Dr. F. A. Sondley of Asheville, referring to the community's history. The bronze chandeliers and furniture were designed by Ellington. Paneling is wire-brushed cyprus, and the floor is travertine.

5. Polychrome terra-cotta pinnacle.

FOX THEATRE

660 Peachtree Street, Atlanta, Georgia, 1925–26, Marye, Alger, & Vinour, architects.

The Fox Theatre was originally designed as the Yaarab Temple of the Ancient Order of the Nobles of the Mystic Shrine; the architects were selected by competition. During construction, funding proved insufficient to complete the building. William Fox ultimately guaranteed the necessary funding to complete construction. The theater maintains exceptional architectural integrity, containing virtually all of the original furnishings and light fixtures.

1

2

1. Women's lounge on the mezzanine.

2. Detail of chair on the mezzanine encircled by a "souk," replete with blue sky.

3. Even the ladies' lounge is lavish; vanity table detail.

4. The theater's proscenium continues the theme of a Moorish city, including Oriental rugs hanging over the walls.

3

4

TEMPLE SINAI REFORM CONGREGATION

6227 St. Charles Avenue, New Orleans, Louisiana, 1933, Moise H. Goldstein with Weiss, Dreyfous & Seiferth, architects.

2

Emile Weil, Inc., was the associate architect of Temple Sinai, a reinforced concrete building.

1. The Perpetual Light and Ark on the Bema are framed by a large brass grille, possibly by the Picirilli Brothers, since the architectural firm was working with them on metalwork for the Capitol. Chandeliers were produced by Tiffany.

2. General view.

3. Bema.

4. Detail of chandelier and geometric stained glass window with a menorah.

3

4

LOUISIANA STATE CAPITOL

Riverside Street at Capitol Lake Drive, Baton Rouge, Louisiana, 1930–31, Weiss, Dreyfous & Seiferth, architect.

2

3

The Lousiana State Capitol building was the result of Covernor Huey P. Long's effort to construct an imposing monument to replace the earlier capitol. Only the second sky-scraper capitol to be constructed, the building was illustrated in *Architectural Forum,* December 1932. The reinforced steel structure is clad in Alabama limestone. Situated on a bluff over the Mississippi River, the capitol faces south, in the direction of the city.

1. General view.

2. Ulric H. Ellerhusen sculpted the pinnacle components; an allegorical figure representing Science inhabits the southeast corner.

3. Low relief stone band of a pelican motif (the brown pelican is the state bird) alternates with a lotus motif. These bands embellish various levels at the base of the capitol, flanking the 48 steps leading to the entrance.

4. Entrance is flanked on the west by *Pioneers,* Lorado Taft's heroic sculpture of an allegorical *Spirit of Adventure* who is surrounded by De Soto and La Salle, a Franciscan friar, Native Americans, a frontiersman, and an American colonist.

1

4

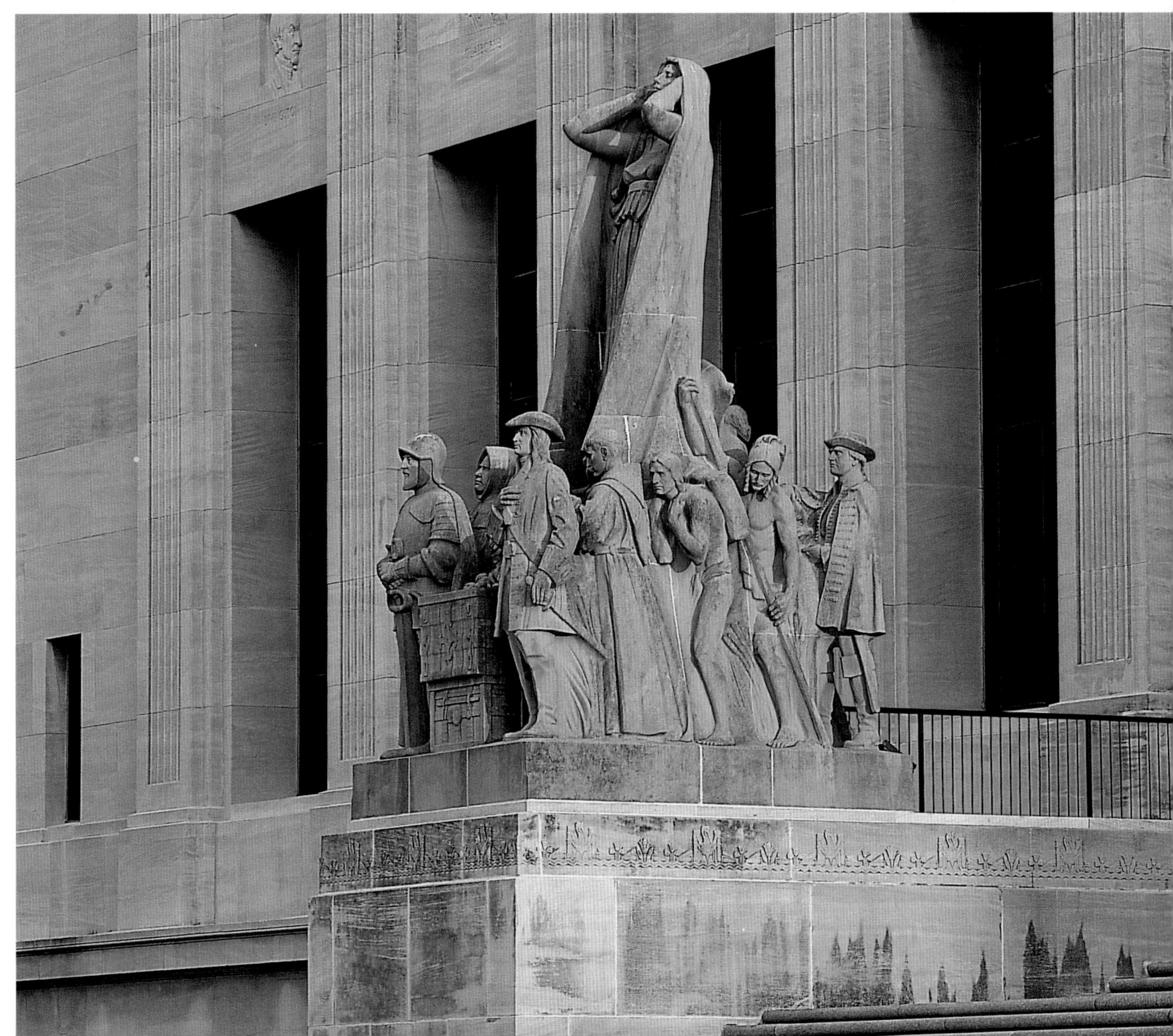

5

6

7

5. Two bronze plaques face the vestibule walls, one illustrating the original capitol building, this one dedicated to the new.

6. Memorial Hall's pilasters are Red Levanto, the floor is Sienna travertine alternating with Yellow Travertine Antique with decorative borders of Cardiff Green, Belgian black marbles and Red Levanto and light green from Vermont. A gift from France in 1934, one of a pair of Sèvres porcelain vases flanks the elevator bank. The bronze elevator doors illustrate the former governors of Louisiana. Solis Seiferth collaborated with the Picirilli Brothers of New York, producing loose working drawings for the door panels, which were translated into models by the Picirillis and cast by the Cellini Company of New York.

7. The west wall of Memorial Hall leads to the Senate Chambers, enclosed by bronze doors relating scenes from Louisiana's history. A bronze cornice is a duplicate of the historical frieze on the exterior with minor changes. Jules Guerin painted the mural *The Abundance of Earth.*

8. House of Representatives contains walnut and Australian laurel wood furniture and bronze chandeliers designed by the architects. The stenciled ceiling is Celotex, a material made from sugarcane. Walls are Crazannes Anteor stone; pilasters are Sienna travertine. Jaune Benou marble is used for wainscoting and door surrounds.

9. First floor plan, *Architectural Forum,* December 1932.

8

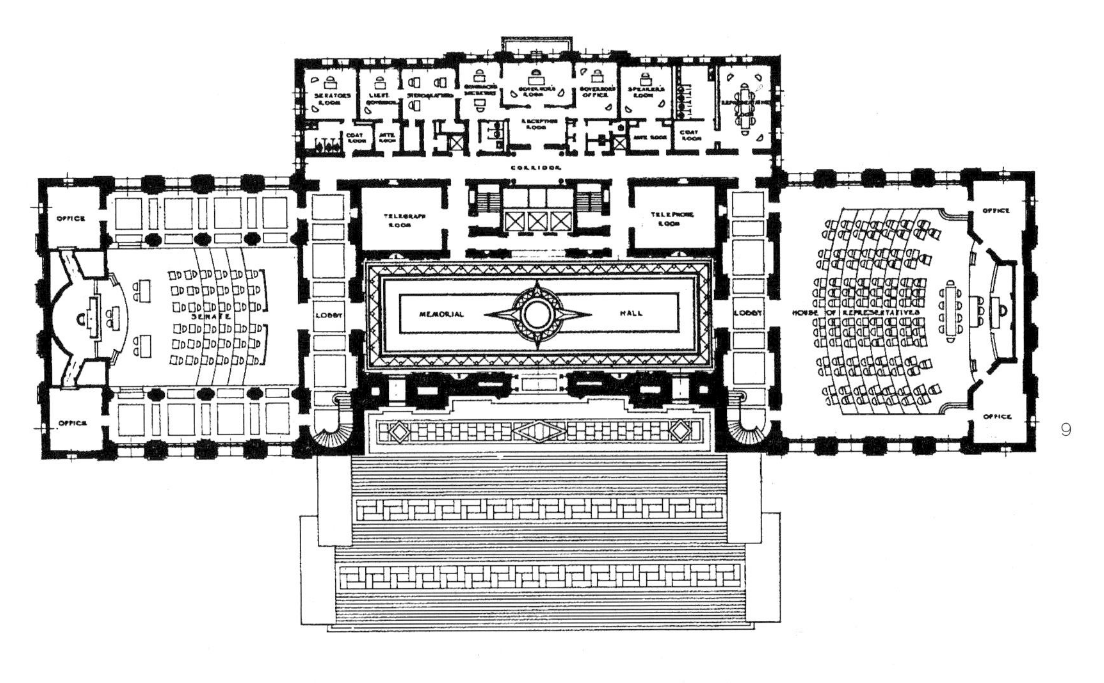

9

THE MIDWEST AND PRAIRIES

In the Midwest, skyscrapers elicited passionate responses. Sinclair Lewis immortalized this aspect of the ballyhoo years in *Main Street, Babbitt,* and other popular novels. The eponymous protagonist of *Babbitt,* George, describes Zenith, a midwestern city which "had between three and four hundred thousand inhabitants now—he could see the top of the Second National Tower, an Indiana limestone building of thirty-five stories. Its shining walls rose against the April sky to a simple cornice like a streak of white fire. Integrity was in the tower, and decision.... As Babbitt stared, the nervousness was smoothed from his face, his slack chin lifted in reverence ... he was inspired by the rhythm of the city, his love of it renewed. He beheld the tower as a temple-spire of the religion of business...."[1]

Every emerging metropolis in the Midwest adopted this highly visible emblem of modernity—the skyscraper. The developers of the Circle Tower building in Indianapolis advertised: "This is the logical business home of those far-visioned executives who are looking toward Tomorrow." Construction of a skyscraper in a midwestern city was a news event. "Circle Tower Is Rising," declared the *Indianapolis Times* of October 3, 1929. The architects, Rubush & Hunter, had been asked by property management firm Klein & Kuhn (now F. C. Tucker Realty Co.) to tour several eastern cities with the property managers to "obtain data to ensure Indianapolis the most modern character of office space."[2] The *National Real Estate Journal* described the marketing campaign for Circle Tower as "unusually attractive" and notable for simply illustrating the building, without its name, in various brochures and newspaper advertisements created by Klein & Kuhn.[3] Circle Tower has a unique, stepped shape (produced by the site, which is located on the corner of Monument Circle), a form easily identifiable. The silhouette was used in advertising as an icon for

Valley National Bank Building,
(Firstar) 512 Walnut Street, Des Moines, Iowa, 1931–32,
Proudfoot, Rawson, Souers & Thomas, architects.

Above. Woodbury County Courthouse, 620 Douglas Street, Sioux City, Iowa, 1918, William Steele with Purcell & Elmslie, architects; Alfonso Ianelli sculpture.

Opposite. Woodbury County Courthouse, John Norton, murals.

luxurious office space. The bronze transom grille over the entrance, bronze doors, elevator doors, and details in the lavishly marble-clad lobby exuded elegance. An additional feature was the inclusion of a built-in wash basin with marble counter in each office suite.

Circle Tower is not an isolated example of the use of a building's design as an advertising strategy. Utilizing logos and design to create corporate identity became a major phenomenon during the 1920s as the power of advertising and the importance of marketing began to be recognized by various industries.[4] Motifs and logos associated with print advertisements were often included in the design elements of modernistic retail and corporate buildings, and vice versa. A skyscraper's silhouette could be perceived as symbolic of a company's prestige, as well as an advertisement for the products or services manufactured or provided by the corporation. Color and modernist design attracted the public's attention by starkly contrasting with surrounding buildings, which were often fussy *Beaux-Arts* confections. Frank W. Blair, the president of Union Trust Company, was one of the first bankers in the country to underwrite commercial aviation, and the modernistic style of the bank's building embodied this commitment to new technologies and the twentieth century. The entrances are surrounded by polychrome terra-cotta, which is used liberally at the base and pinnacle of the Union Trust building to attract attention. The architect, Wirt C. Rowland, stated, "We no longer live in a leisurely age, nor do we move on streets from which it is possible to contemplate and enjoy minute sculpted detail. What we see we must see quickly in passing, and the impression must be immediate, strong and complete. Color has this vital power."[5]

Unusual and bold design could produce a distinctive building as much as the use of color. The monolithic Chicago Daily News building was an imposing and prescient structure on the Chicago River. The first skyscraper in the United States to incorporate a public plaza into the design, the Daily News was also the first structure in Chicago to utilize a novel solution of site and zoning restrictions by purchasing air rights from the Chicago Union Station Company.[6] Conveyance of air rights allowed unused space above Chicago Union Station to be transferred to the Daily News building, permitting the new construction to exceed the zoning envelope.[7] Anne Lee, reviewing the Daily News building for *The Architectural Forum*, described the engineering feat of building a foundation among eight subterranean railroad tracks. Caissons, watertight chambers in which underground construction takes place, were sunk between the tracks without once interfering with the operation of the trains.[8] Designed by Holabird & Root, the Daily News building consists of twenty-five floors faced with limestone on a base of polished granite. Alvin W. Meyer created the ornament carved into the limestone, which portrayed the history of writing and the printing industry. Motifs in the Midwest were often derived from industry, especially automotive, although the region's economy also had a strong agricultural component. The Rand (now Dain) Tower in Minneapolis, Minnesota, celebrates Rufus Rand's passion for aviation (he was a member of the Lafayette Escadrille, an elite World War I air corps unit), which is evident in the

ornamental details: prop planes hover over the Marquette Avenue entrance. In Auburn, Indiana, the Auburn Automobile Company built an administration building containing a showroom. A. M. Strauss, architect of the showroom, employed the modernistic style to promote the increasingly popular mode of transportation, the automobile. Modernistic design now signified a company's commitment to "progress," which was increasingly defined as the availability and ability to purchase consumer products. Cars, radios, and refrigerators were transforming American lives. To produce these appliances and vehicles, industrial production had vastly increased after World War I, made possible as a result of technological advances. For example, passenger cars in service increased—from 6,771,000 in 1919 to 23,121,00 in 1929.[9] By identifying with industry and technology, the architects and designers of art deco appealed to the beneficiaries of these efforts, the consumers.

Merchandise Mart,
200 World Trade Center
Chicago, Chicago, Illinois,
1930, Graham, Anderson,
Probst & White; lobby mural,
Jules Guerin.

Medinah Athletic Club (Hotel Intercontinental), 505 North Michigan Avenue, Chicago, Illinois, 1929, Walter W. Ahlschlager, architect.

Ironically, despite their reaction against industrial production, participants of the Arts and Crafts Movement, active in Detroit and other cities in the Midwest at the turn of the century, offered antecedents to modernistic design. Simple geometric ornament was viewed by these artists as an expression of democracy, if not theosophical concepts. American transcendentalism had become widespread, counteracting mechanization and industrialization. The influential 1918 Woodbury County Courthouse in Sioux City, Iowa, an early modernistic public building, is a synthesis of these concepts. A reviewer for *The Western Architect* described the effect of the courthouse as "Serene, almost impudent.... You feel a sense of illusion about its reality which leaves you presently to be followed by the feeling that the building itself is the only reality and its surroundings are phantoms. Unconsciously you find yourself eliminating the incongruous environment and see the building surrounded by a kind of Elysian field from which [sic] goes up to the unclouded Iowa sky...."[10] William A. Steele collaborated with William Gray Purcell (each had worked in the office of Louis H. Sullivan early in their careers) and George Elmslie. Flat planes, a component of Prairie style, were introduced; ornament was sublimated to form. The ornament itself was restrained, in lower relief and less bombastic than historical styles. Alfonso Ianelli's sculptures, flanking the severe entrance, merge into the building's components, becoming integrated into the structure. While it was the architects' originality which produced such a significant public building, the influence of the Arts and Crafts Movement's emphasis of geometric motifs cannot be underestimated.

The Arts and Crafts Movement also caused artists and architects to reconsider the geometrical ornament used by Native Americans and found on historic and contemporary artifacts. In the Midwest, Chippewa, Ojibwa, and other Eastern Woodlands Indians produced quilled and (after the advent of European traders) beaded ornament on their leather garments.[11] The modular quality of these materials was manifested in decorative patterns which tended to be highly stylized. A major example of the influence of Native American motifs in midwestern modernistic architecture is the Naniboujou Club on Lake Superior. Named for the Cree deity of nature, it is a unique tribute to native cultures inhabiting this region of northern Minnesota. Naniboujou was initially conceived on a grand scale. A promotional brochure (written, designed, and printed by the Stewart-Taylor Company in Duluth, Minnesota, 1928) described the proposed club as follows: "Swim in the swimming pool, go round eighteen holes or take on a tennis set; come in for dinner.... In spite of its wilderness location, the telephone is at your elbow...."[12] Although the vision described by the brochure was enticing, few memberships were actually sold. Numerous celebrities had been offered free memberships, which the board of trustees had imagined might induce less exalted individuals to participate. Ring Lardner was notorious for remarking that he was a member, and intended to spend time there as soon as he learned how to pronounce Naniboujou (Nani'-bou-jou).[13] Construction began in the spring of 1928, and the entire complex, including a dock on Lake Superior, the tennis courts, and a golf course, was estimated to cost $350,000. Ultimately, the golf course, tennis courts, and swimming pool for the lodge were not built, victims of the economic depression following the Wall Street crash on October 27, 1929. The *Cook County News-Herald* of Grand Marais frequently reported on the club's progress. An article dated August 9, 1928, titled "Work at Club of Naniboujou Progressing," described the construction site: "Contractor Dinsmore had seven carloads of materials on site and numerous workers. Architect Holstead informs us that the lobby—which as you were previously informed will be 70 feet long—will be a marvel of 'art nouveau.' The color effect of the walls will be the latest creation of architectural art, full sized French doors, and the beautiful furnishings will present to you the finest lobby in the Northwest."[14] The Art Nouveau influence is difficult to discern. Perhaps Holstead was actually inspired by the Secession architecture and design found in Vienna, a subsequent movement which had many characteristics similar to art deco.

Naniboujou's opening was described by the *News-Herald:* "[The interior is] richly finished in brilliant colors that are not at all unpleasant to the eye. The drapes and furniture all conform to the scheme of the whole." The giant fireplace at one end of the large reception room provided a cozy atmosphere, and four hundred people were served at dinner.[15] A period photograph includes slot machines in the dining room. Since Prohibition was still enforced, the club's proximity to Canada may have facilitated access to alcoholic beverages as well.

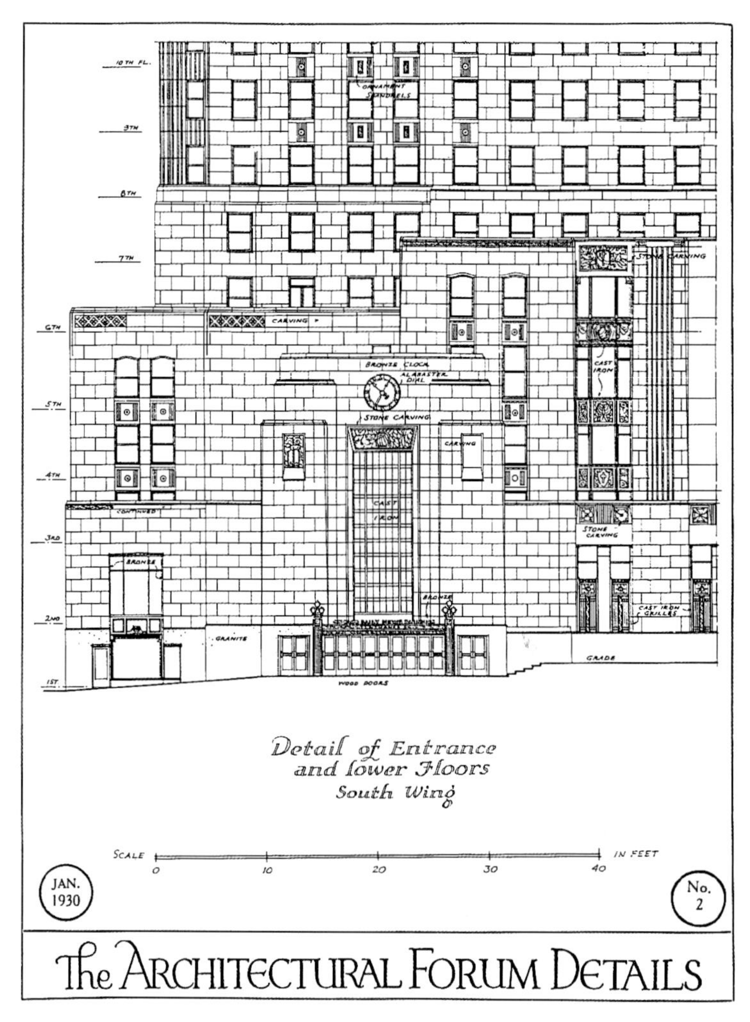

Daily News Building, 2 North Riverside Plaza, Chicago, Illinois, 1929, Holabird & Root, architects, elevation drawing.

However flamboyant the scene at Naniboujou, Prohibition reflected the political will of various midwestern religious communities. Despite this, religious freedom has been associated with the Midwest since the early nineteenth century, when various Utopian communities were built. Inspired by the Utopian ideals of Robert Owen (founder of New Harmony, Indiana), Joseph Smith, prophet and founder of the Church of Jesus Christ of Latter-day Saints, embarked on an ambitious building program in the Midwest. By the 1920s modernistic churches were being constructed in every region of the United States, but few are as opulent as the Shrine of the Little Flower in Royal Oak, Michigan, devoted to Saint Thérèse of Lisieux. Saint Thérèse's veneration of Christ compelled her to enter a convent when she was fifteen. She died only nine years later of tuberculosis. Her inspirational writing, in which she referred to herself as "insignificant as a tiny flower" in the garden of God, was published after her death and proved to be enormously popular. Saint Thérèse's canonization by Pope Pius XI in 1925 inspired the infamous Reverend Charles E. Coughlin to build a shrine, constructed with donations solicited via the National Radio League of the Little Flower.[16] The decorative details and ecclesiastical art in the Shrine are sumptuous evidence of Reverend Coughlin's successful fund-raising efforts. Numerous artists were supported by their ecclesiastical work during the 1920s and 1930s, and the bountiful iconography of the Catholic church provided myriad opportunities for the visual arts.

Opposite top. S. H. Kress Store, 120 North Main Street, Hutchinson, Kansas, 1930, Edward F. Sibbert, architect.

Opposite bottom. Daily News Building, general view.

Public buildings were another important source of work for artists and sculptors during the Depression. Courthouses, city halls, and schools characteristically included a decorative-arts program. A new form of public building also emerged. As cities and industries expanded, large municipal auditoriums and convention centers for trade shows, theater, sports, and symphonies became as essential as skyscrapers. Kansas City, Missouri, ideally situated as a hub for the region, built an ambitious program: an auditorium, sports arena, and small ballroom under one roof, all accessed through an expansive lobby. For the grand opening, a brochure was printed in which the author declared that the structure was built in "a dignified monumental style that is strictly modern without being freakish."[17] This concern with a restrained expression of style is typical of midwestern art deco. Generally, color is not flamboyant and sculptural programs are subdued.

The Prairie region, while similar to the Midwest, has a different natural environment, which influenced the art deco motifs devised by local architects. Modernistic buildings abound, ranging from major skyscrapers and public buildings to small commercial buildings in farming communities. An alluring feature of these buildings is the predominant use of the Prairie's environment and cultures as a basis for ornamental motifs and even structural elements. The grassy plains of Nebraska, Kansas, and the Dakotas, aside from supporting a variety of wildlife and vast herds of buffalo, yielded a unique building material. Cut into modular, stackable elements, sod formed a functional building material for the pioneers. Banked into low hills or arising directly from the earth, these sod houses were vernacular expressions of what later evolved into the Prairie style of Frank Lloyd Wright, Walter Burley Griffen, and George Maher. Wright's seminal essay "In the Cause of Architecture," published in *The Architectural Record* in 1908, proclaims: "The prairie has a beauty of its own and we should recognize and accentuate the natural beauty, its quiet level."[18] Indigenous culture and environment frequently inspired the ornamental motifs found in Wright's early residential work in Chicago.

Native American and regional motifs are a significant component of the decorative program for the Nebraska State Capitol. The Nebraska legislature voted to build a new capitol building in 1919, and architect Bertram Good-

hue was selected by competition for proposing a novel design.[19] Dispensing with the usual dome, Goodhue designed a skyscraper. Nebraska's capitol building became the first in the United States to embody the modernity of the twentieth century. Hartley Burr Alexander, a historian and professor of philosophy at the University of Nebraska, as well as the author of *The Pictorial and Pictographic Art of the Indians of North America,* suggested a concept for the capitol's decoration. Lecturing on the topic "Nebraska as the Theme for an Artist," Alexander suggested that maize should be a "symbol of the life of the State."[20] He continued, "Then the Indians—the first men in this region, with their ritual of the calumet, the bearers of the first seed corn and the ceremony of Hako—should be remembered. And last, the procession of white men—French trappers, Lewis and Clark, the Jesuits, the Mormons, the 49ers, the United States Army, the cowboys, the surveyors, the railroad builders; and the pioneers with the prairie fires, the blizzards, the drouths, the grasshopper infestations, their barn raisings; the pioneer miracle which transformed the virgin prairies into farms and homes, churches and schools in one generation—should be illustrated within the Capitol."[21] The Capitol Commission became interested in his ideas, and in February 1922 he was introduced to Bertram Goodhue. Alexander's first assignment involved writing inscriptions for specific spaces. Above the capitol's main entrance, one of his statements reads, "The Salvation of the State is Watchfulness in the Citizen." His involvement in the building's decorative program increased, and ultimately he collaborated with the artists, actually suggesting particular motifs and designs. It was Alexander's idea that the sculptor Lee Lawrie carve *cavo-relievo* panels portraying bison to flank the steps leading to the capitol's main entrance. Alexander's contribution to the Nebraska capitol building was so effective that Goodhue asked him to collaborate with his firm on the Los Angeles Public Library.

Pickwick Theater, 5 South Prospect Park, Park Ridge, Illinois, 1928, Harold Zook, architect. Rendering, *The Western Architect,* November 1929.

Bertram Goodhue had a genius for building simple, modern geometrical forms; however, he continued to endorse the *Beaux-Arts* ideal, integrating art and architecture. One of the major artists he worked with on the capitol, in addition to Lee Lawrie, was Hildreth Meiere, then a young, unknown artist. While working on this commission, Meiere was also collaborating with Goodhue on the dome of the National Academy of Sciences in Washington, D.C. Unfamiliar with Meiere, the Nebraska Capitol Commission asked Goodhue for her credentials; he responded that she was the artist working on the Academy of Sciences; and when confronted with an identical query by the building committee for the Academy, Goodhue explained that she was the mosaic artist for the Nebraska State Capitol.[22]

The repercussions of a decorative program evolving from regional inspiration were rapidly apparent. The McDonalds, who had already designed the Joslyn Memorial in Omaha, Nebraska, in an *École Beaux-Arts* style, decided to revise their plans and sought Alexander's participation. This decision caused dissension on the project when Alexander decided to amend the subject matter of David Brcin's sculptural panels.[23] Other buildings influenced by the Nebraska State Capitol include Wichita North High School; the United States Courthouse in Wichita, Kansas; and the Boston Avenue Methodist-Episcopal Church in Tulsa, Oklahoma. The County Courthouse in Oklahoma City contains decorative elements which have historical and cultural significance. A white man greeted by a Native American, an encounter consistently, but duplicitously, romanticized as peaceful, is a recurring theme in regional American art deco architecture and appears on the architrave above the south entrance of the courthouse. The Oklahoma County Courthouse is the most ornate of the buildings comprising a Civic Center that includes an auditorium and the City Hall/Municipal Building. Designed by Solomon Layton and George Forsyth, a firm (with Jewell Hicks as a partner from 1925 through 1935) specializing in the design of public and commercial buildings, the 13-story Oklahoma County Courthouse recounts local historical events in architectural ornament and murals.[24]

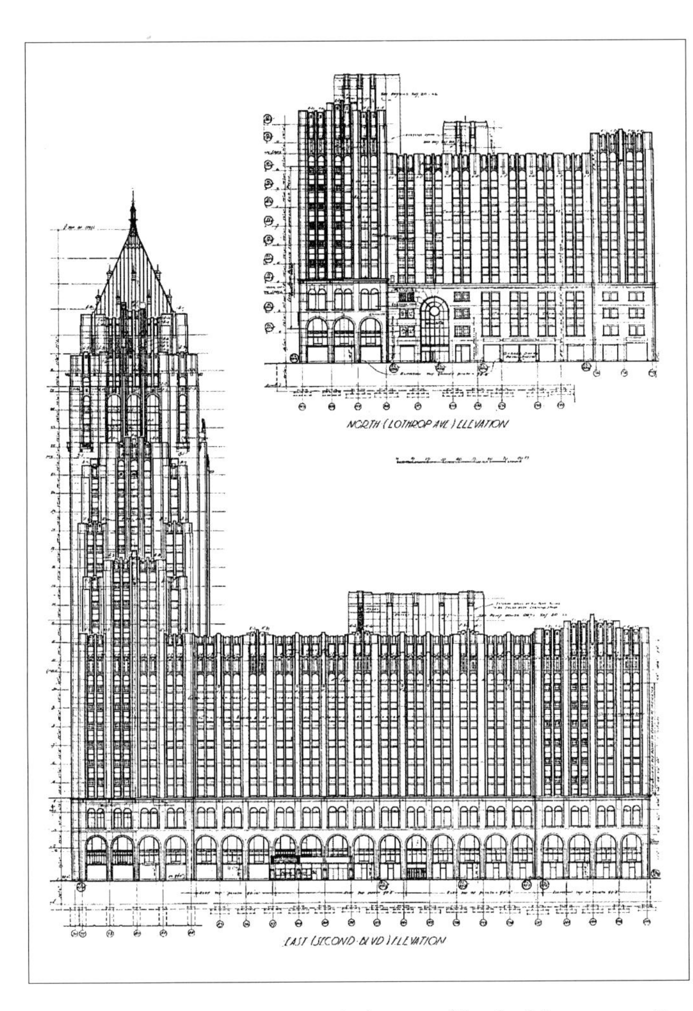

Fisher Building, 3011 West Grand Boulevard, Detroit, Michigan, 1928, Albert Kahn, architect. Elevation drawing, *The American Architect*, February 20, 1929.

The 1926–29 Boston Avenue Methodist-Episcopal Church in Tulsa, Oklahoma, was designed by Bruce Goff, associated at that time with Rush, Endacott & Rush. Adah M. Robinson's claim to be the originator of the design is problematic.[25] Clearly the design for the church was an obvious evolution in Goff's work during the 1920s, especially when the faceted tower of the Boston Avenue Church is compared to a 1922 elevation drawing of a hypothetical cathedral.[26] According to a letter written by Audrey Cole, the wife of the chairman of the building committee, dissatisfaction with proposals submitted by several architects (prior to Rush, Endacott & Rush's participation) led her to ask Adah M. Robinson, a graduate of the Art Institute of Chicago and an art educator in Tulsa, for suggestions.[27] Robinson gave the Coles a rough sketch. Excited by her conception, the building committee asked for drawings. Since Robinson was not an architect, she asked a former student, and the architect of her residence, Bruce Goff, who was working with the architectural firm Rush, Endacott & Rush, to assist her. According to the church's version of events, Goff's preliminary sketches of the church were a coherent expression of Robinson's initial concept, and she is considered the architect. However, viewed in the context of his previous work, the church was clearly a component of a body of work that is distinctively Goff's. When the contract to construct the Boston Avenue Methodist-Episcopal Church was drawn up, Robinson was included as supervisor of the building's decorative program. In this capacity she executed large-scale drawings for brilliantly colored stained glass in the sanctuary, and designed motifs for ornamental details, such as the polychrome terra-cotta praying hands and stylized flowers.[28] She worked with the sculptor Robert Garrison, another former student, to create the circuit riders over the north and south entrances. In addition to the dramatic decorative scheme, the Boston Avenue Methodist Episcopal Church was the first ecclesiastical building to be designed for an emerging automobile culture. A porte cochere accommodated passengers arriving by car, and generous parking space was provided.[29]

Art deco churches, municipal buildings, skyscrapers, and small commercial buildings in the Midwest and Prairie regions are evidence of a national desire to exemplify modernity. By combining the usual art deco motifs—zigzags, stepped pyramids, and stylized flowers—with motifs specifically related to the region, architects and designers were affirming that particular city or region's commitment to progress.

KOGEN-MILLER STUDIOS

1734 North Wells Street, Chicago, Illinois, 1928–32. Edgar Miller, architect/artist; Sol Kogen, developer/contractor.

1

2

3

Edgar Miller and Sol Kogen created an artist's haven from crumbling Victorian houses, which they rebuilt in an individualistic art deco style. Materials for the studios were often constructed from recycled bricks with string courses of remnant and found tiles. Relief sculpture over the entrance of R. W. Glasner's house was illustrated in *Architecture,* August 1932. The structure, owned by Mark C. Mamolen, is currently under restoration.

1. Entrance to 1734 North Wells, carved by Edgar Miller.

2. 155 Carl Street, west elevation, rough sketch by Edgar Miller, *The Western Architect,* December 1930.

3. Interior of one building with modeled plaster ornament.

4. Miller was a versatile artist and responsible for the majority of details, such as this carved wood grille running from the first to the third floor.

4

5

5. The dining room is illuminated on the east wall by Miller's most brilliant stained glass work.

6

6, 7, 8. Details of stained glass in dining room. Miller etched into the paint on glass with ferrous sulphate, which would be tempered for permanence.

7, 8

9. Detail of stained glass window on east wall.

magnificent

UNION CARBIDE AND CARBON BUILDING

230 North Michigan Avenue, Chicago, Illinois, 1928–29, Burnham Brothers, architects.

2

3

4

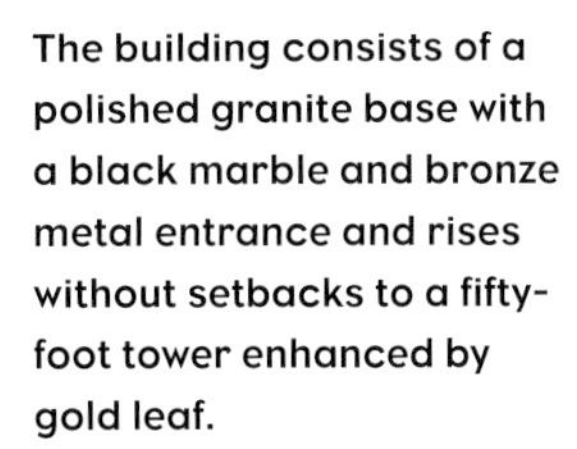

The building consists of a polished granite base with a black marble and bronze metal entrance and rises without setbacks to a fifty-foot tower enhanced by gold leaf.

1. General view.

2. Detail of corner at setback.

3. The exterior is faced with green terra-cotta with gold pier caps and coping, illustrated in *The Western Architect*, April 1930. The tower culminates in a fifty-foot-high pinnacle.

4. Detail of bronze ventilation grille in lobby.

5. Mezzanine.

5

1

MUNDELEIN COLLEGE

(Loyola University) 6525 North Sheridan Road, Chicago, Illinois, 1929, Joe W. McCarthy of Chicago and Nairne W. Fisher of Dubuque, Iowa, architects.

1

2

3

4

Clad in gray Indiana limestone, the college was illustrated in *Stone*, November 1930.

1. The archangel Jophiel (*The Beauty of God*) guards the Tree of Knowledge with a flaming sword.

2. Foyer grille with the sky-scraper motif representing the school's building.

3. Mundelein College/Loyola University, chapel niche with stained glass.

4. General view.

BLOOM HIGH SCHOOL

101 West Tenth Street, Chicago Heights, Illinois, 1931, Royer, Danelli & Smith, architects.

Bloom High School is a reinforced concrete structure clad in buff brick with cast stone pier caps and coping. The modernistic school has a formal entrance flanked by statues by Felix O. Schlag, which were donated by the class of 1936.

1. Entrance.

2. Detail of statue.

3. Cast stone pediment over the entrance transom grille has an etched texture.

2

3

1

PARAMOUNT THEATER

23 East Galena Boulevard, Aurora, Illinois, 1931, Rapp & Rapp, architects.

1

2

3

The Paramount Theater is situated on the Fox River. A marquee tower is heavily embellished with polychrome terra-cotta. The current marquee is a duplicate of the original.

1. The murals were carefully cleaned during restoration and needed little retouching. The stenciled foil, however, is entirely reproduced using the original motifs for stencils; restoration was meticulously performed by the Conrad Schmidt Studio.

2. Polychrome terra-cotta detail.

3. Consisting of 1,885 seats originally, the theater was the first air-conditioned building in Aurora.

4. General view.

4

PARAMOUNT
PARAMOUNT ARTS CENTRE TICKETS ON SALE NOW
CALL BOX OFFICE AT 630 896 6666

MADAME C. J. WALKER BUILDING

617 Indiana Avenue, Indianapolis, Indiana, 1927, Rubush & Hunter, architects.

The Madame C. J. Walker Building is a four-story reinforced concrete flatiron, multifunctional building designed to serve as the African American community's social and cultural center. The theater provided the African American community an opulent environment in which to view Hollywood movies, a welcome alternative to being relegated to "Colored Only" balconies. Built to memorialize Madame Walker, the first black woman in the United States to amass a fortune, the building contained the Madame Walker Beauty College, offices, beauty salon, meeting rooms, dance areas, and the 1500-seat theater.

2

3

4

1. Ornamental polychrome terra-cotta on the exterior may have been modeled by Alexander Sangernebo, the sculptor of the Indiana Theatre's exterior ornament, also designed by Rubush & Hunter. An Estonian, Sangernebo studied at the Industrial Arts School in Hamburg prior to emigrating to the United States in 1888. He was chief designer of the Indianapolis Terra Cotta Company in the 1890s, then opened his own studio in Brightswood, and later in Indianapolis.

2 Sphinxes flanking the stage were modeled by Joseph Willenborg, a sculptor who worked with the firm on other buildings. Willenborg emigrated from Munster, Germany, in 1923 and was employed by William Herman & Sons, a decorative-arts company in Indianapolis during the 1920s.

3. East elevation detail of the terra-cotta cornice ornament and coping manufactured by the Indianapolis Terra Cotta Company.

4. Glazed plasterwork in the foyer.

CIRCLE TOWER

5 East Market Street (situated on the corner of Market Street and Monument Circle), Indianapolis, Indiana, 1928–29, Rubush & Hunter, architects.

1

Circle Tower is faced with Indiana limestone in compliance with a 1922 plan for the Circle determining height and materials. Circle Tower was the first commercial structure in Indianapolis to utilize modern setbacks and conform to 1922 zoning ordinances.

1. White terra-cotta details emphasize setbacks. Terra-cotta was manufactured by the Indianapolis Terra Cotta Company, a subsidiary of American Terra Cotta and Ceramic Company. Alexander Sangernebo was chief designer for Indianapolis Terra Cotta.

2. Elevator doors are gold-tone bronze and were manufactured by the Tyler Company. Lobby walls are polished Italian marble; terrazzo floor.

3. Lobby is quite intact except for minor renovations.

4. Foyer.

5. The ventilation grille in the foyer was designed by sculptor Joseph Willenborg, who trained at William Herman & Son, an interior decoration firm specializing in plasterwork.

6. Polished pink granite contrasts with the bronze transom screen also designed by Willenborg. Rubush & Hunter seem to have been under the influence of Egyptomania. The header and grille are soft Etruscan gold luster, executed by the Michaels Art Bronze Co., Covington, Kentucky, who displayed the building as an advertisement in *The Architectural Record*, February 1931.

2

3

4

5

CIRCLE TOWER
55
MONUMENT
CIRCLE
5 E MARKET ST
All Deliveries
STARBUCKS
COFFEE

SmithGroup
SmithGroup

UNION TRUST BUILDING

(Guardian Building) 500 Griswold Street, Detroit, Michigan, 1927–28, Wirt C. Rowland of Smith, Hinchman & Grylls, architects.

2

Forty stories high, the Union Trust Building was documented in the November 1929 issue of *The American Architect.* Colored brick cladding the exterior was developed by Wirt C. Rowland and ultimately marketed by the manufacturer as "Guardian Brick," an unusual choice of material, since limestone generally sheathed skyscrapers at the time. The incorporation of color was significant. According to Rowland, "We no longer live in a leisurely age, nor do we move on streets from which it is possible to contemplate and enjoy minute sculpted detail. What we see we must see quickly in passing, and the impression must be immediate, strong and complete. Color has this vital power."

3

1. The lobby is clad with tiles manufactured at Pewabic Pottery. Mary Chase Stratton, ceramic artist, produced the tiles used on the interior and exterior. Lobby walls are of Belgian black marble, red Numidian marble, and Mankato stone. A mezzanine leads to the former banking room, now the offices of the architectural firm Smith, Hinchman & Grylls.

2. Entrance to banking room. Forty thousand pounds of Monel metal, an alloy of approximately two-thirds nickel and one-third copper, was utilized to produce the grille surrounding the bank's entrance, elevator doors, tellers' grilles, the Monel clock, and check-writing desks. The grille, laminated by welding sheets together in layers, was illustrated in *The Metal Arts,* January 1929. The Monel was produced by Gorham Co., Providence, Rhode Island; Favrile glass from Tiffany is inlaid on the elevator doors.

3. Ezra Winter painted the mural on the east wall of the banking room, *Map of Michigan,* illustrated in *Architecture,* June 1929. The banking room's barrel vault ceiling was designed by Thomas DiLorenzo.

5

6

7

4. Detail of pinnacle in the form of interlocking hexagons, with angles alternately 60 and 30 degrees. Union Trust was built by Frank W. Blair, one of the first bankers in the United States lending to commercial aviation.

5. South elevation; the stepped pyramid in various permutations forms another leitmotif on the exterior. The Union Trust Building was illustrated in *Stone*, June 1929. Booth Brothers Hurricane Isle and Somes Sound and Clark's Dark Montrose granites were used for a base on the first floor line; stories two through six of the exterior were faced with a select Minnesota limestone known as Yellow Ledge Mankato. Atlantic Terra Cotta produced the facade material.

6. Detail of ornament on exterior, south elevation.

7. Exterior detail, south elevation.

NATIONAL SHRINE OF THE LITTLE FLOWER

2123 Roseland Avenue, Royal Oak, Michigan, 1929–33, Henry J. McGill, architect.

1

2

The National Shrine of the Little Flower was illustrated in *Pencil Points*, September 1935. Indiana limestone sculptures on the tower were created by Rene Chambellan, who worked closely with Henry J. McGill as the plan evolved from a more traditional spired church form. The pinnacle is in the form of a crown, symbolizing the Kingdom of Heaven, entwined with mustard plant flowers. Sculpture on each corner represents one of the four writers of the gospel, symbolized by man, lion, calf, and eagle (Matthew, Mark, Luke, and John). The figures at the granite base surrounding Christ are Mary and John the Apostle on one side, Mary Magdalene, and the centurion Longinus, with his lance. Small stone grilles at the bases of these statues originally concealed loudspeakers for broadcasting Reverend Coughlin's sermons. The base of the tower was designed to be an outdoor pulpit, formed from five stone slabs carved with images of the archangels. The features of the archangel Michael are actually those of the archbishop of Detroit at the time, Bishop Michael Gallagher, and the shield contains the seal of the diocese of Detroit.

1. Monel and bronze doors and transom grille are the work of Corrado Giuseppe Parducci.

2. The National Shrine of the Little Flower was founded by the controversial Reverend Charles E. Coughlin in 1925. The money for this lavish art deco church was solicited via radio broadcast. Donor response was substantial and the church basement was designated a Royal Oak Post Office substation to process all of the mail. The National Radio League of the Little Flower, as a tribute to donors, included a carved stone of each state's name and official state flower, which are scattered over the exterior.

3. The Shrine's altar is one slab of Carrara marble; carved peacocks ornament the sides, a motif derived from the Byzantine period, referring to the shedding of plumage annually and the opulent regrowth, giving rise to the legend that the peacock's flesh is incorruptible.

4. Patinated bronze roof and aluminum lantern and parapet caps are surmounted by a gold cross.

5. A Roman soldier, Longinus, pierced Christ's flesh, and when a drop of blood spurted into his eyes, he was cured of cataracts and converted to Christianity. His dedication to building cathedrals is symbolized by the edifice on the hilt of his sword.

6. Gold-finished brass and Monel transom grilles designed by McGill in collaboration with Parducci utilize extruded and die-stamped elements.

7. Oak doors carved by Alois Lang are embellished with chased brass and were featured in *Architecture*'s "Portfolio of Church Doors," February 1934. Panels with angels are cast and enameled bronze.

8. Rendering of the Shrine courtesy of Drawings and Archives, Avery Architecture and Fine Arts Library, Columbia University.

9. Plan of the Shrine, illustrated in *Pencil Points*, September 1935.

5

8

6

7

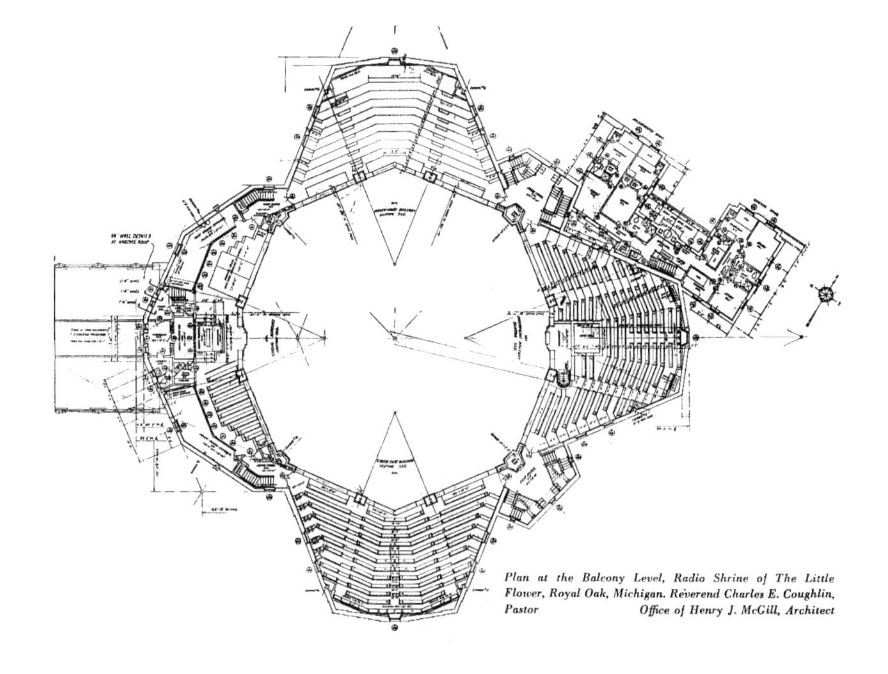

Plan at the Balcony Level, Radio Shrine of The Little Flower, Royal Oak, Michigan. Reverend Charles E. Coughlin, Pastor *Office of Henry J. McGill, Architect*

CRANBROOK

1221 North Woodward, Bloomfield Hills, Michigan, 1929–31, Eliel Saarinen, architect.

1

Cranbrook is composed of numerous buildings. The Academic Building and Tower (currently Hoey Hall) is reinforced concrete faced with brick. The dome originally contained an observatory.

1. General view of the Quadrangle, Hoey Hall and Tower.

2 The Junior Dormitory (now Marquis Hall), 1927; Page Hall, 1929–30; and the Senior Dormitory (now Stevens Hall), 1927–28.

3. Géza Maróti, a Hungarian sculptor, worked with Saarinen, designing the pergola terminals on the steps leading up to the pergola.

2

3

4. Dining Hall, containing furniture designed by Saarinen.

5. Alumni Court, detail of column capitals.

LIVINGSTON MEMORIAL LIGHTHOUSE

Lakeshore Drive, Belle Isle, Michigan, 1930, Albert Kahn, architect.

1

2

The lighthouse was built on the northern point of Belle Isle as a memorial to William Livingston, known as "Sailor Bill," former president of the Lake Carriers Association. Illustrated in an advertisement for Carborundum Products in *Stone,* the lighthouse is fabricated from white Georgia marble; carborundum wheels were used in cutting the marble fluting and ornament at the Marietta plant of the Georgia Marble Company.

1. Pinnacle and lantern.

2. Detail of cast-bronze door.

3. General view.

4. Lighthouse entrance; sculpture by Géza Maróti.

3

4

WILLIAM
LIVINGSTONE

NANIBOUJOU CLUB

(Naniboujou Lodge) 20 Naniboujou Trail, Grand Marais, Minnesota, 1928–29, Holstead & Sullivan, architects.

1

Naniboujou was romantically conceived as a luxurious resort on Lake Superior. The site is one of the few along the lake with any beach, and the building was constructed on a bed of sand and pebbles, which provided excellent drainage. Naniboujou Club was illustrated in *Trails of the Northwoods*, Winter 1928. Groundbreaking for the Naniboujou clubhouse was attended by Grand Portage Indians, who danced in costume; a blessing was provided by medicine men in the Ojibwa language. Frank H. Piquette, a Chippewa from Red Lake, was spokesman and interpreter for Mike Flat, Grand Portage chief. More than two thousand people attended the groundbreaking, then the largest gathering ever in Cook County.

1. Original light fixture on a balcony, which was added later.

2. Original shutters ornamented with Eastern Woodland flower motif; the shingles cladding the exterior are also original.

3. Exterior light fixture above entrance to Dining Hall.

4. General view.

2

3

4

5. The interior of the Dining Hall is virtually intact, painted by artist Antoine Gouffee. Naniboujou is the Ojibwa deity of nature and inspired the ornament. Weighing two hundred tons, the massive fireplace of native stone is the largest in Minnesota and is supported by a deep footing. The curtain hoops and furniture are original. A false ceiling above the Dining Hall conceals space for a catwalk between it and the roof, and the shape may be reminiscent of a canoe used by the Cree or Chippewa Indians in the region. Chandeliers were constructed with parchment and delicate wood tracery. The lightweight construction indicates that these fixtures may have been prototypes and intended to be cast in bronze, but because of the 1929 crash on Wall Street were never executed.

6. The curtain hoops are recessed into the false ceiling of Celotex. The painted ornament is derived from Cree, Ojibwa, or other Eastern Woodlands ornament, which originally would have been executed in woven quill or beaded work.

7. Original buffet table in Dining Hall.

8. Original Dining Hall furniture was carved with stylized Ojibwa motifs.

6

7

8

THIS CAR UP
EMPLOYEES OF
KANSAS CITY POWER AND LIGHT COMPANY
IN MILITARY SERVICE
1917 - IN WORLD WAR - 1919
THOSE WHO DIED FOR FREEDOM
THOSE WHO LIVED TO ENJOY THE BLESSINGS OF LIBERTY

KANSAS CITY POWER & LIGHT BUILDING

1330 Baltimore Avenue, Kansas City, Missouri, 1930–31, Hoit, Price & Barnes, architects.

2

3

4

The building is a skyscraper whose dominant motif from pinnacle to interior details is the sunburst of radiant energy.

1. The lobby features Monel elevator doors and ventilation grillework with terrazzo tile floors; illustrated in *Architecture*, October 1934.

2. Ornamental band of cast stone above black marble window transoms.

3. General view.

4. Monel mailbox in elevator lobby.

COMEDY
Orch
RC

KANSAS CITY MUNICIPAL AUDITORIUM

211 West Thirteenth Street, Kansas City, Missouri, 1933–34, Alonzo H. Gentry, Voscamp & Neville, Hoit, Price & Barnes, architects; Erwin Pfuhl, structural engineer; W. L. Cassell, mechanical engineer.

2

A multifunctional space containing an arena, Music Hall, Exhibition Hall, and Little Theater, the auditorium was constructed to capitalize on the city's central location in the Midwest. The building was published in *Architectural Forum*, March 1937.

1. *Winter*, one of four murals in the Orchestra Promenade entitled *Four Seasons*, analogous to the stages of life and painted by Walter Alexander Bailey.

2. The equivalent of a ten-story building, the auditorium encompasses an entire city block.

1

3

4

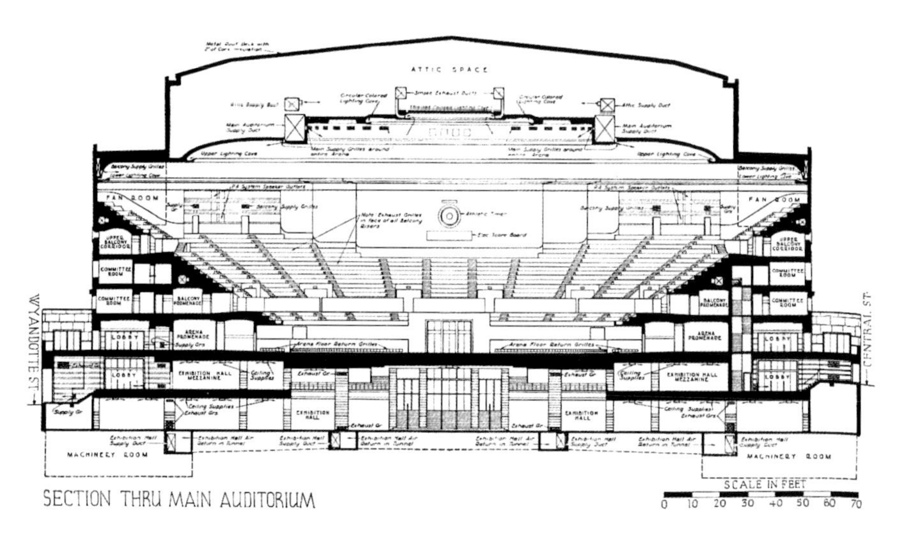
ATTIC SPACE
FAN ROOM
COMMITTEE ROOM
LOBBY
EXHIBITION HALL
MACHINERY ROOM
WYANDOTTE ST
CENTRAL ST
SECTION THRU MAIN AUDITORIUM
SCALE IN FEET
0 10 20 30 40 50 60 70

5

3. Flanked by two panels illustrating the four seasons, the twenty-seven-foot-high mural *Mnemosyne and the Muses (Science, the Plastic Arts, Music, and Literature)* was painted by Ross Braught on location.

4. Mezzanine view of the Orchestra Promenade; metalwork throughout the Auditorium was designed by Homer Neville.

5. Section drawing, *Architectural Forum*, March 1937.

6. The grand stairway to the Kansas City Philharmonic Orchestra's Music Hall, accessed from the Grand Foyer (as are all spaces in the Municipal Auditorium), is clad with gray and golden Sienna marble interspersed with bands of Rellante and Breche Orientale marble.

JOSLYN ART MUSEUM

2200 Dodge Street, Omaha, Nebraska, 1928–31, John and Alan McDonald, architects.

1

2

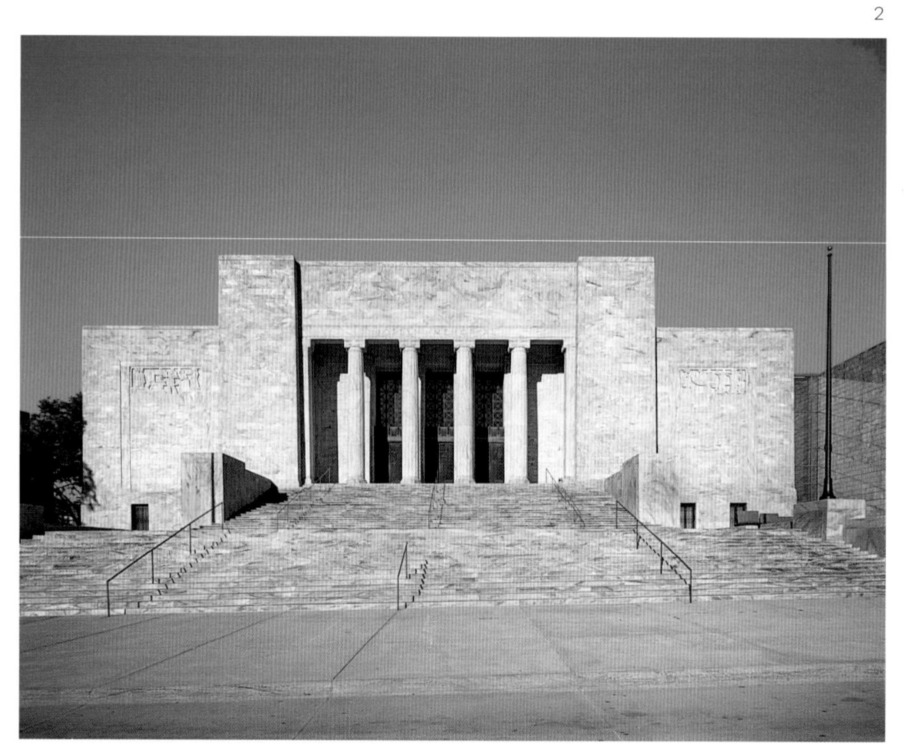

3

4

5

The Joslyn Art Museum was originally intended to be in the *Beaux-Arts* style. A Moderne revision was accomplished by architect Herschel Elarth, engaged by the McDonalds at the suggestion of Thomas Kimball. Not all elements could be redesigned in the modernistic mode, such as grilles and doors which had already been cast. The west elevation entrance (the primary entrance is on the east) was illustrated in *Architecture,* February 1933. Hartley Burr Alexander, who had worked with Bertram Goodhue on the decorative scheme for the Nebraska State Capital Building, worked with the McDonalds on the Joslyn. His knowledge of anthropology, regional history, and philosophy contributed to the use of quotes, as well as the decorative panel themes on the exterior.

1. *Indian Prayer for Life* and the other sculpture panels were carved from John David Brcin's full-scale plaster models by Edward and Gino Ratti. Brcin's work was illustrated in *American Architect,* April 1929.

2. General view. George Joslyn was the founder of one of the largest newspaper services in the world, Western Newspaper Union. Joslyn established the Great Western Type Foundry and Western Paper Company, which provided syndicated copy on ready-to-print plates for newspapers.

3. Various Beaux-Arts elements were unchanged in the Moderne revision, such as this bronze grille, produced by the General Bronze Corporation. Thunderbird wing sconces flanking the grilles were designed by Walter Kantack and illustrated in *The Kaleidoscope,* January 1930.

4. Low-relief cast-bronze doors designed by John David Brcin. The museum's entrance and other elevations were illustrated in *The Architectural Record,* June 1932.

5. A steel-reinforced structure, clad with Georgia pink or Etowah Fleuri marble, riders on rearing horses were originally intended to flank the steps to the entrance. Column capitals on the portico were envisioned by Elarth as a fusion of classical tradition with the expression of indigenous Native American culture.

JOSL
IN REMEMBRANCE OF
GEORGE ALFRED JOSLY
ALERT CITIZE
OF THE PRES
LIBERAL
THIS BUILDING IS GIVE
FOR THE
BY SARAH

6

7

8

6. Lobby walls, ceilings, and pilasters are Roman travertine; Paul Manship's bronze sculptures, *Indian Hunter* and *Pronghorn Antelope*, flank the entrance to the Floral Court.

7. Thunderbird motif of peroba wood is inlaid in the Reception Room's wainscoting. All lighting fixtures in the museum were designed and produced by Walter Kantack. The chandeliers in the lobby were featured on the cover of a magazine published by Kantack, *The Kaleidoscope*, January 1930, and featured in an article describing the process of working with the architects to produce appropriate illumination for the museum. The two large lanterns in the lobby are bronze with aluminum reflectors to produce indirect light.

8. Floral Court walls are clad with Virginian Aquia stone. Originally covered by a skylight, the Floral Court has since been enclosed. Trim surrounding the door and windows is Vert Antico marble from Greece. The fountain is clad in faience and the floor tiles are Pennsylvania Moravia.

9. Mezzanine surrounding the lobby is supported by columns of a black and gold marble from the Italian island Palmaria.

NEBRASKA STATE CAPITOL

Fifteenth Street at K Street, Lincoln, Nebraska, 1919–32, Bertram G. Goodhue, architect.

2

The Nebraska State Capitol was the first American skyscraper capitol building. *American Architect,* October 1934, devoted the entire issue to the Capitol.

1. Grand Foyer. Tiles on the dome were influenced by Bertram G. Goodhue's interest in Mexican architecture. White Utah onyx set in tracery of White Colorado Yule marble stained a light amber, executed by Sunderland Brothers Company, illuminates the Rotunda and the Grand Foyer.

2. Grand Foyer; Hildreth Meiere worked on the ceiling and pendentive mosaics in the Grand Foyer. Transverse arches portray labor, law, public spirit, and religion; "interesting realism" was achieved using modern dress.

3

4

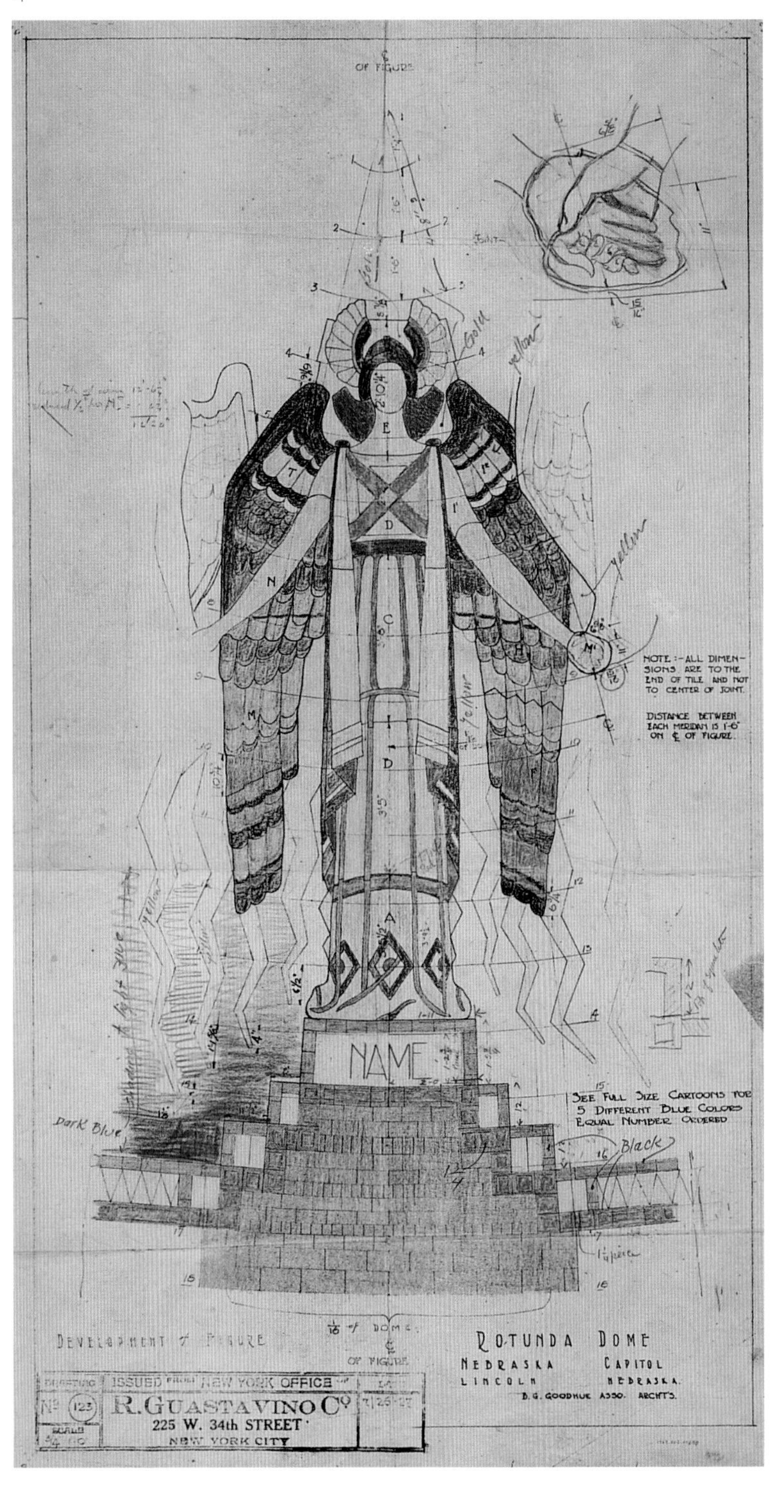

5

6

3. Lee Lawrie's doors to the Senate Chamber are four inches thick, hinged by bronze through-bolts screwed into the bronze frame. The bronze handles on the Senate doors were designed by Howard Swenson, who took two weeks to make the design for the foundry.

4. Meiere's cartoon for the mosaic figures in the Rotunda was drawn over-scale to compensate for shrinkage, one-half inch to one foot. Once the tiles were manufactured, they were assembled in the factory and shipped to the construction site. The cost of building the Capitol was so extensive that elements of the decorative program could not be completed until the 1960s. Drawing, Guastavino/Collins Collection, Drawings and Archives, Avery Architecture and Fine Arts Library, Columbia University.

5. One of three sibyls, past, present, and future. Vestibule dome sun forms the crown, surrounded by the four seasons and the signs of the zodiac; the second concentric band depicts the fruits of the soil—cattle, sheep, maize, wheat, grasses, fruits, and flowers.

6. Meiere used decorative concepts from Plains Indian beading; the four pendentives illustrate plowing, sowing, cultivating, and reaping. In 1928 Meiere received a gold medal in mural decoration from the Architectural League for decorations of Nebraska.

7

7. *Mercy Before the Law,* engaged figures, sculpted by Lee Lawrie, merge into simple pylons.

8. Section and tower plans, *American Architect,* October 1934.

9. Detail of Lawrie's *The Spirit of the Pioneers,* above main entrance. During his collaboration with the architect and artists, Hartly Burr Alexander wrote, "I am anxious to see the capitol speak a language which will be fresh and interesting now and will remain so in the future."

10. Detail of frieze over the main entrance.

11. *The Sower,* reproduced in *Art & Archeology,* September 1933, is cast bronze and weighs 8.5 tons, including the bronze base.

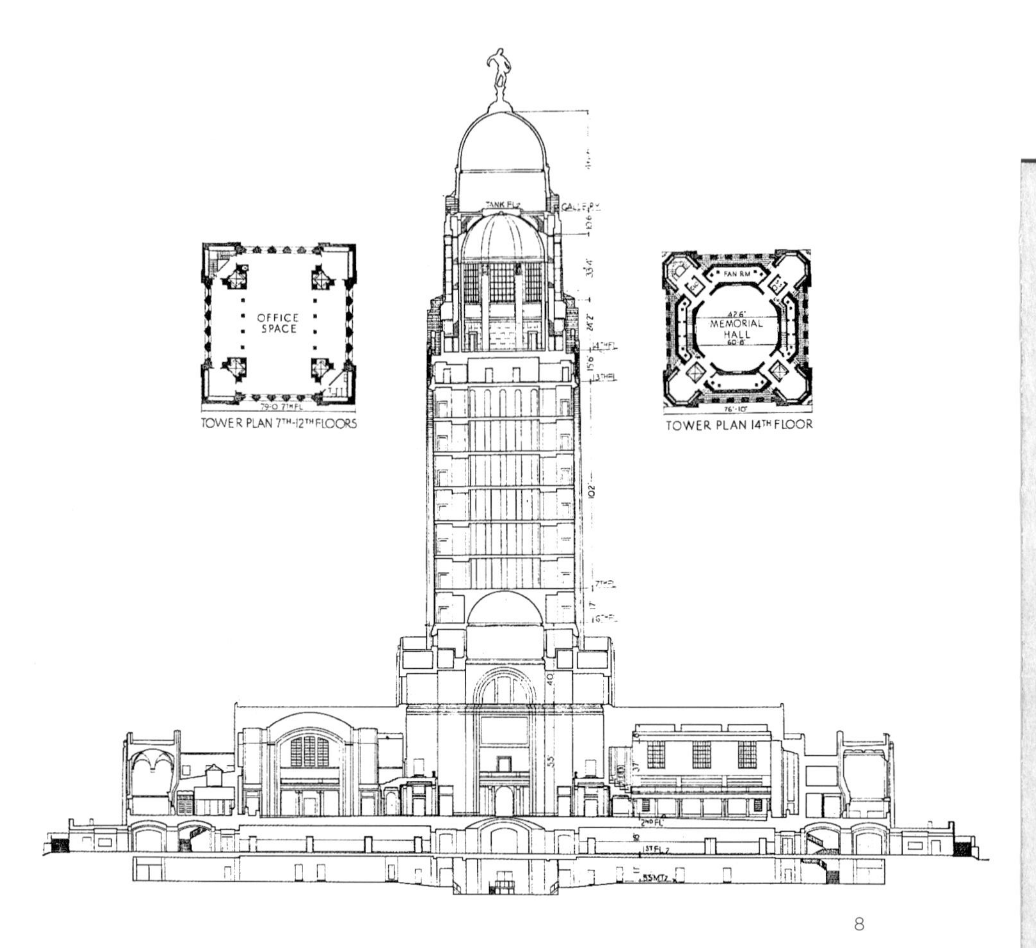

8

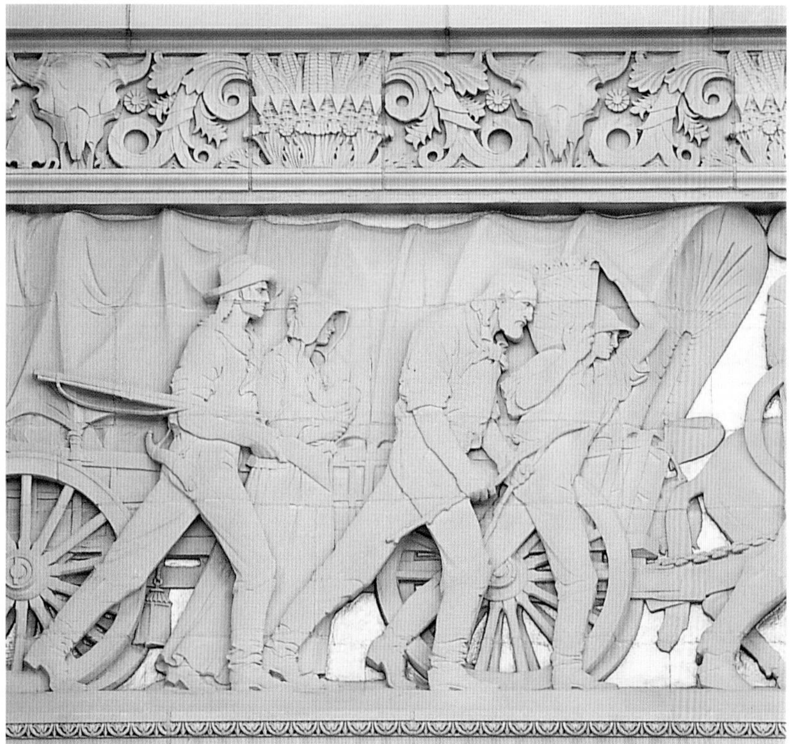

9

10

WICHITA HIGH SCHOOL

(Wichita North High School), 1437 Rochester Avenue, Wichita, Kansas, 1929, Glenn Thomas, architect.

1

2

Wichita High School was deemed to be a noteworthy example of the "prairie" style according to the WPA's *Kansas: A Guide to the Sunflower State.* Built on the edge of the Little Arkansas River, nearby Minisa Bridge was designed by Bruce Moore (the sculptor who designed the terra-cotta ornament on the school) to harmonize with the school. Dedicated in 1932, the bridge's name was selected by the students, who chose the title from a composition by Thurlow Lieurance, an authority at the time on Native American music.

3

4

1. Pinnacle of tower.

2. Wichita High School is constructed of buff brick, with coping of polychrome terra-cotta.

3. Drawing of Wichita High School from the 1930 yearbook. The first yearbook on completion of the school contained the dedication: "The noble tower of our building symbolizes to every student and teacher of Wichita high School North, visions and aspirations of pioneer years. It recalls the heroic idealism of the past and pledges us to the beauty and success of the future."

4. Interior stairwell of the school.

5

5. Detail of polychrome terra-cotta band below the coping, composed of bison, sunflowers, and tipis separated by an angular motif.

6. Polychrome terra-cotta friezes by Bruce Moore appear over the east and south entrances. The friezes are flanked by piers capped by polychrome Plains Indians. Moore was a significant sculptor whose work *Panther* illustrated an article regarding the opening of the Whitney Museum of American Art in *American Magazine of Art*, February 1932.

AD ASTRA PER ASPERA

UNITED STATES FEDERAL BUILDING AND COURTHOUSE

401 North Market Street, Wichita, Kansas, 1932, Louis A. Simon, architect.

1

The United States Federal Building and Courthouse is a five-story steel and concrete building clad with sanded and carved Bedford limestone. Originally containing the post office, the building was illustrated in *The Architectural Forum,* September 1931.

1. General view.

2. Carved limestone parapet detail; an ear-of-corn motif refers to the regional agriculture.

2

3

4

3. A stylized sunflower, the state flower of Kansas, and ears of corn are motifs sculpted in limestone.

4. Cast-iron spandrels portray a Plains, possibly Kiowa, warrior to commemorate the western heritage.

5. Cast bronze with gold-finish eagles above the vestibule in the ground-floor lobby.

6. Cast-bronze ventilation grille in courtroom.

7. The courtroom was restored in 2000 and retains numerous original details, including the furniture. Eighteen types of marble were used for the floors and walls in the courtrooms, lobbies, and halls. Twenty-three-carat gold leaf was applied to the cast-plaster coffered ceiling. The presiding judge's bench is faced with marble and centered with a diamond-shaped slab imported from Germany. The tapestry walls are original.

5

6

7

BOSTON AVENUE METHODIST CHURCH

1301 Boston Avenue, Tulsa, Oklahoma, 1926–29, Bruce Goff of Rush, Endacott & Rush; Adah M. Robinson, artist.

1

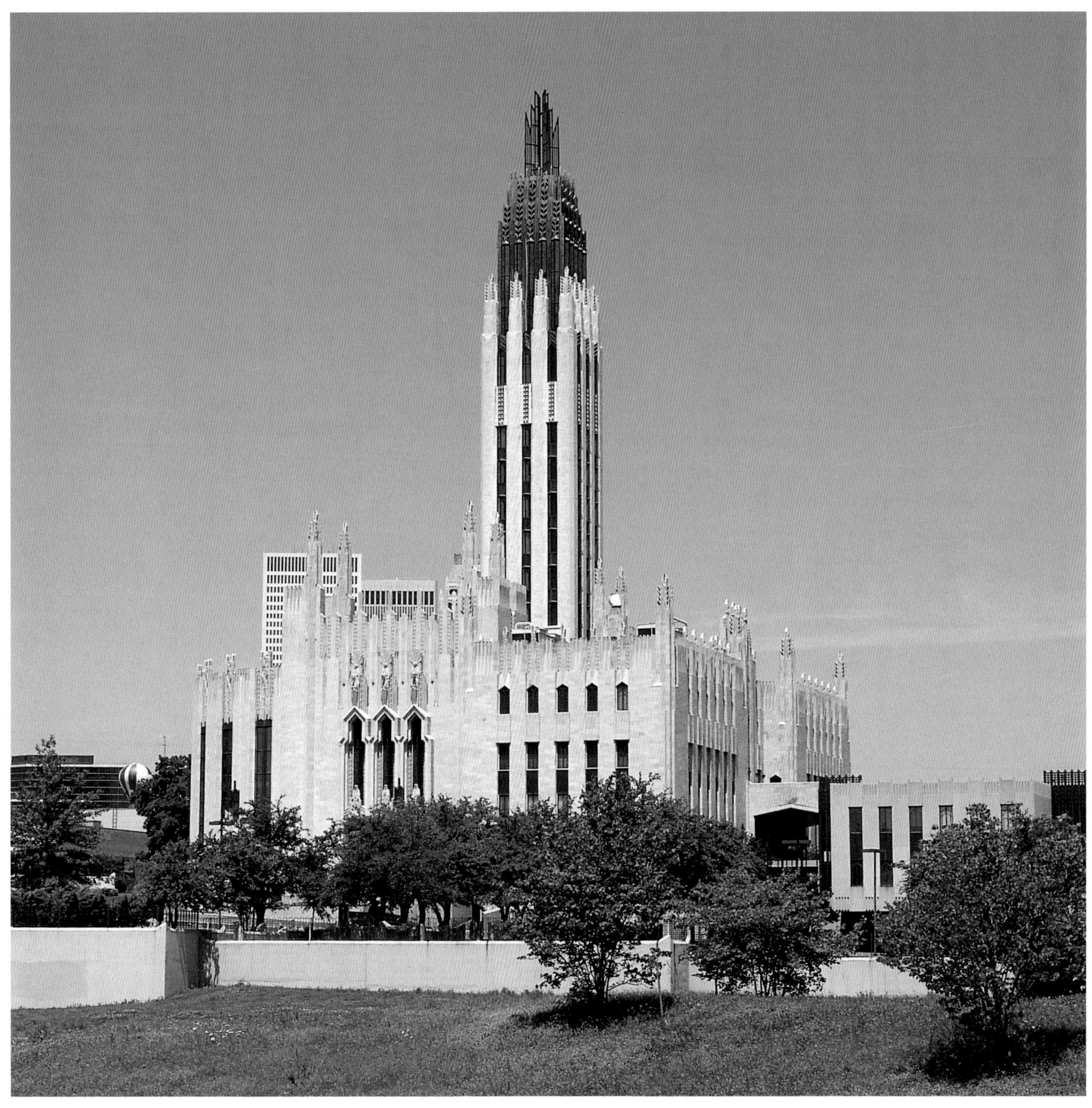

The church was constructed from Indiana limestone; the steel frame tower has a copper and glass lantern. The complex includes a sanctuary, small chapel, and offices; the lobby serves as a social center. Terra-cotta finials on the auditorium represent the critoma, or torch lily, a local flower Robinson perceived as symbolic of the generosity of the Methodist faith. The seven point star symbolizes seven virtues—patience, purity, knowledge, suffering, kindness, love, and truth.

1. General view.

2. John Wesley, the founder of Methodism, is the central figure above the north entrance. To his right is Susanna Wesley, his mother, and to his left is his brother, Charles Wesley.

2

3

3. Spire and faceted lantern.

4. "Circuit Riders," sculpted by Robert Garrison and located above the south entrance, is a tribute to the men whose valor and aggressiveness spread the Methodist religion. The central figure is a composite, while the rider on the west, or to the central figure's right, is Francis Asbury, appointed by John Wesley as the first superintendent of the faith. The figure on the east is William McKendrie, the first American bishop.

5. A group of figures kneeling with clasped hands symbolize qualities such as sacrifice.

6. The colors used in the sanctuary were termed by Robinson as "atmospheric" and all sight lines lead to the pulpit.

4

5

FAIRGROUNDS PAVILION

Tulsa State Fairgrounds, Tulsa, Oklahoma, 1933, L. I. Shumway, architect.

2

The Fairgrounds Pavilion is reinforced concrete clad with buff brick. *Atlantic Terra Cotta* devoted the January 1928 issue to promoting the use of terra cotta for smaller and less expensive buildings. The Coliseum on the State Fair Grounds in Tulsa illustrated the uses of Atlantic Terra Cotta Company's Abbochrome material for the frieze, panels and inserts of entrances, pier caps, and coping.

1. Polychrome terra-cotta architraves appear above the entrances.

2. East elevation.

3. Detail of terra-cotta.

3

1

WILL ROGERS HIGH SCHOOL

3909 East 5th Place, Tulsa, Oklahoma, 1938, Atkinson, Senter & Koberling, architects.

1

2

3

Will Rogers High School is a two-story buff brick structure. A Cherokee cowboy, Will Rogers segued from being an actor in the 1920s and 1930s to a syndicated columnist and humorist. Although he dropped out of high school, Rogers and his myriad accomplishments inspired students.

1. Terra-cotta spandrels.

2. Terra-cotta details.

3. Coping and terra-cotta details.

4. Vestibule.

5. Entrance.

4

5

WILL ROGERS
HIGH SCHOOL

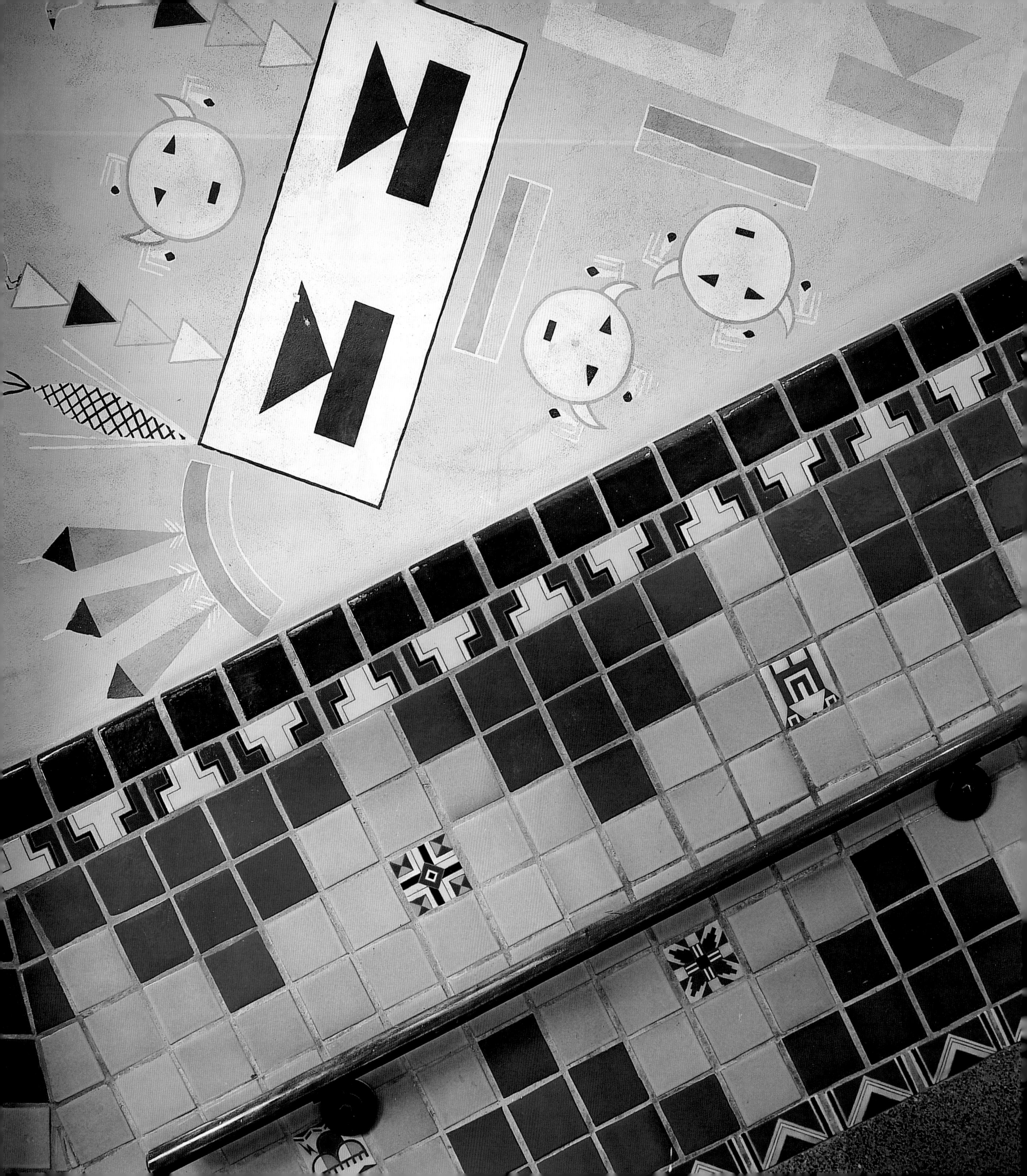

THE SOUTHWEST

Buffalo dancers emerge and begin the ceremony in the plaza of Taos Pueblo, located in northern New Mexico. East of the Pueblo, the jagged Sangre de Cristo mountain range is covered with snow in January, when the sacred Buffalo Dance occurs. Invoking sympathetic magic by wearing buffalo hides and headdresses, the Pueblo's participants solemnly perform this annual ritual, despite the disappearance of buffalo herds after the advent of railroads, which were built when the United States acquired Arizona and New Mexico from Mexico. Taos Pueblo's culture and rituals remained virtually intact, however, surviving the Spanish and, later, the American presence.

After conquering Mexico, Spanish explorers continued north, trekking through harsh deserts and over rugged mountains. Francisco Vásquez de Coronado arrived at Zuni Pueblo in 1541, in what is now New Mexico, only to discover an aboriginal village composed of loosely scattered adobe buildings, and that the inhabitants had none of the precious metals the Spanish had found in Aztec and Mayan cities.[1] The Anasazi culture had already abandoned its sophisticated masonry complexes such as Chaco Canyon for these smaller villages by the time the Spanish Crown had organized a formal *entrada*. Missions, consisting of churches and subsidiary structures, were established at the Pueblos along the Rio Grande. Application of the Baroque style (dominant in Spain and Mexico) to these missions was impossible due to constraints of materials, labor, and expertise, resulting in the evolution of a generic Spanish mission style. A convergence of Pueblo and Spanish architecture was achieved through simplifying construction and decorative elements and adapting adobe technology.

McKinley County Courthouse, 201 West Hill Street, Gallup, New Mexico, 1934, Trost & Trost, architects. Lloyd Moylan, funded by the WPA, painted the murals in the lobby, inspired by Kiva paintings. Kivas, subterranean spaces where religious rituals are performed, continue to be an integral element of Pueblo architecture and culture.

The cubistic volumes found in Pueblos and Spanish missions appealed to early modernists, who emphasized modular ornament and geometric elements. "The architectural forms which had arisen in the American Southwest in the eighteenth and early nineteenth centuries—a blend of the Indian and provincial Spanish architecture from Mexico—had long held a fascination for the American from the eastern sections of the country. In the more openly eclectic work of the nineteenth century, it was only a short step from admiration of a past historic form to the desire to employ the form in a contemporary building."[2] Regionalism, manifested in the arts and architecture of the Southwest, was an appealing concept to American artists and architects who were searching for a definition of national identity. By 1900, images of the Native American and related historical events were considered to be the ideal symbols of American identity, embodying both the exotic and the indigenous. Painters and photographers believed that the Indian's relationship to nature offered an antidote to rapid industrialization and urbanization in the United States.[3] The motifs used by the Pueblo, Navajo, and Apache cultures were predominantly angular and, when figurative, highly schematized and easily assimilated into the modernistic idiom. Rose Henderson, an architectural critic writing in the 1920s about Native American cultures and their impact on art and architecture, quoted a Taos painter who stated, "The Indians were the first cubists in this country."[4]

The Watchtower, Grand Canyon, Arizona, 1932. Mary J. Colter, architect. The Hopi Room on the ground floor of the tower was painted by Hopi artist Fred Kabotie, portraying traditional myths. The galleries above the ground floor were painted by Fred Geary, an artist working with the Harvey group. Mary Colter was prescient, working with Native American artists to create a Pueblo Deco style.

For the general public, exposure to the Southwest frequently occurred as a result of traveling. The Atchison, Topeka & Santa Fe Railroad exhorted "See America First," and artists were commissioned to create brochures and posters for the railroad depicting the magnificent southwestern landscape inhabited by exotic native Indians.[5] The impact of the AT&SF Railroad's advertising campaign is evident—E. Irving Couse painted *Osage Village*, one of three lunettes in the new (1926) Missouri State Capitol building; Ernest L. Blumenschein, Oscar Berninghaus, and Bert Phillips, three other painters from the nascent art colony in Taos, also contributed to the Capitol's decorative program. All four artists had produced paintings for AT&SF Railroad brochures and other visual advertising.[6] The artists living in Taos at the turn of the century tantalized the public with their paintings of the awesome landscape, traditional architecture, and Pueblo life. Referring to the art colony in Taos, Rose Henderson wrote, "Artists made their homes and studios in ancient adobe houses that with very few changes became most satisfactory living quarters. They studied the Indian's symbolism, his dramatic ceremonial dances, his unmatched vigor and variety of decorative design."[7] Henderson discussed the impact of these artists on modernistic architecture: "Spanish influence refined and amplified without corrupting this unified simplicty [of Pueblo architecture], and under the lead of American painters,

Opposite. General view of the Watchtower.

DEDICATED TO THE PIONEERS
STATE OF TEXAS
ROSS S. STERLING
BOARD OF REGENTS
A. B. MAYHEW
HENRY PAULUS
WILL HAYES
THOMAS H. BALL
J. W. FITZGERALD
JOHN E. HILL
H. L. KOKERNOT
W. C. CRANE
WEBB WALKER
J. A. HILL
RITTENBERRY & CARDER
W. FRANK LITLE

Opposite. Panhandle Plains Museum, 2503 Fourth Avenue, Canyon, Texas, 1932, E. F. Rittenberry, architect.

American builders and decorators have learned lessons of daring and of restraint."[8]

Fred Harvey's services were a feature of the AT&SF Railroad. Harvey's "innovation" was to provide edible food for train passengers.[9] By 1910 Fred Harvey and company had popularized travel in the Southwest (Arizona, California, New Mexico, Utah, and Texas) by recognizing the importance of "packaging" the unique experience of the region. He built restaurants and hotels which resembled the adobe architecture of Spanish missions and offered guided tours of the Grand Canyon, Pueblos along the Rio Grande, and other sites.[10] Mary Jane Colter, Harvey's designer, and the railroad's architect, Charles F. Whittlesey, designed the 1902 Alvarado Hotel, adjacent to the Spanish-Mission style depot in Albuquerque, New Mexico. Although built in the same style, the hotel contained an Indian Room resembling the interior of a Pueblo abode. Navajo eyedazzler rugs hung on the walls; Hopi kachinas, Acoma pottery, Apache baskets, and silver and turquoise jewelry abounded, among the items tourists might purchase.[11] Colter understood how the cubistic forms of Pueblo and Hispanic architecture could be juxtaposed with geometric ornament inspired by Native American motifs. Harvey contributed an additional flourish—actual Isleta Pueblo women, in print dresses and fringed shawls, who sold their arts to tourists on the steps of the Alvarado.

Right. Panhandle Plains Museum, prickly pear cactus motif runs along the parapet; cougar sculpture.

Trading posts became an adjunct to tourism, where Pueblo Indians, Navajo, and Apaches could sell or trade jewelry, baskets, and textiles, which could be purchased by tourists. Maurice M. Maisel built a trading post in the central business district of Albuquerque in 1937. When he engaged John Gaw Meem, one of the preeminent Pueblo-style architects, Maisel explained to him that he "was not content with the usual conventional Indian thing."[12] Meem made notes regarding the commission and wrote, "It was agreed finally that my preliminary study was to be along the lines of a strictly modern structure, using where necessary Indian symbols."[13] The result of Meem's sketches is a recessed lobby forming a T-shaped display area with windows which are semihexagonal at the corners. A mural above the windows was designed and supervised by Olive Rush, an instructor at the prestigious American Indian Art Institute in Santa Fe. It introduced an element of authenticity rare in Pueblo deco. Pablita Velarde, Pop Chalee, and Harrison Begay are among the nine artists who worked on the mural; each artist was responsible for a specific panel.[14] Black Carrara glass at the base of the building was etched with silver avanyus, a stylized serpent motif found on San Ildefonso pottery.

Panhandle Plains Museum, carved limestone portrait of a cowboy; terra-cotta transom panel of regional cattle brands.

While Spanish Pueblo revival became the dominant stylistic paradigm in New Mexico, and in 1905 became the official style for buildings on the University of New Mexico campus, the Spanish Colonial style was more popular in Texas and Arizona. Phoenix was rapidly expanding in the early twentieth century. Luhr's Tower, an art deco skyscraper with Spanish Colonial details, and other large commercial buildings were being built around Patriot Square. The Los Angeles firm of Morgan, Walls & Clements designed the Valley Bank Professional Building in Phoenix. Trost & Trost was a major firm in El Paso, and designed the O. T. Bassett Tower (published in *The Western Architect*, August 1930) and the Plaza Hotel there, both incorporating modernistic elements.[15] Trost & Trost's McKinley County Courthouse in Gallup, New Mexico, exemplifies their fusion of regional vernacular with modernistic ornament.

Dallas, meanwhile, was developing the Texanic style. The concept for a centennial celebrating independence from Mexico was proposed by Governor James S. Hogg in 1900. Every city was vying to become designated the official location. Hoping to locate the exposition on the existing State Fair grounds, in the early 1930s Dallas businessmen incorporated as the Texas Centennial Central Exposition Corporation. Architect George L. Dahl was involved in this group. The corporation subsequently achieved a political coup: competing with San Antonio, Houston, and Austin, Dallas was ultimately selected as the host site for the primary celebration of the Texas Centennial of Independence. To accommodate new construction on existing Texas State Fair grounds, an additional 180 acres were purchased.[16] Since Dahl had been active in the selection of Dallas, he was given the commission of Centennial architect. Paul Philippe Cret was design consultant. Dahl, when asked by the committee why Frank Lloyd Wright had not been included, responded, "Dallas could either have an exposition or Frank Lloyd Wright," not both.[17] There is little doubt that this repartee was perfectly justified. In 1925, the architect of the Arizona Biltmore Hotel, Albert Chase McArthur, bought the patent rights for the textile concrete block from Wright, a patent which Wright did not own. Wright also claimed credit for the design of the Arizona Biltmore, although he was merely a consultant for four months.[18] For example, an advertisement for Portland Cement featuring the Arizona Biltmore in an April 1930 issue of *The American Architect* included Frank Lloyd Wright's name with the credits.

United States Courthouse, 501 Tenth Street, Fort Worth, Texas, 1933, Paul P. Cret, architect.

George Dahl had been a fellow at the American Academy in Rome after graduating from Harvard. He became a partner in Herbert M. Green's office in Dallas and designed numerous buildings during the 1920s, including collaborating with Cret on buildings for the University of Texas.[19] He is credited with designing the first drive-through bank. Unlike previous expositions, Dahl conceived of these exposition buildings as permanent. Dahl was a pioneer in fast-track design, and construction on the Centennial buildings began before the final design was finished.[20] An advertisement for Incor 24-hour cement appeared in *American Architect* in September 1936, proclaiming that for construction of the monolithic tower and entrance, "'Incor' provided working strengths at least five days sooner than ordinary concrete on each pour; 'Incor' piling for the Hall of State, cast and driven during late Fall, overcame cool weather curing delays, reduced form costs, saved many days on driving schedule," by eliminating nonproductive days waiting for concrete to harden.

Numerous architects, including Donald Nelson, who had contributed to Chicago's Century of Progress, collaborated with Dahl on the exposition, and the critics were enthusiastic: "Out of the Texas Centennial will come an architecture which reflects the cultural development of an empire and its people; an architecture with the feeling of the Aztec expressed in simple lines, an architecture with the touch of the ancient and the classical in the massive pylons and terraced effects; an architecture with the Latin-American feel of romance and golden sunshine; and withal, an architecture that is as modern as Texas is."[21] Pierre Bourdelle, the son of the widely recognized French sculptor Emil Antoine Bourdelle, was one among the myriad major artists who worked on the decorative program. He felt that "If

UNITED STATES COURT

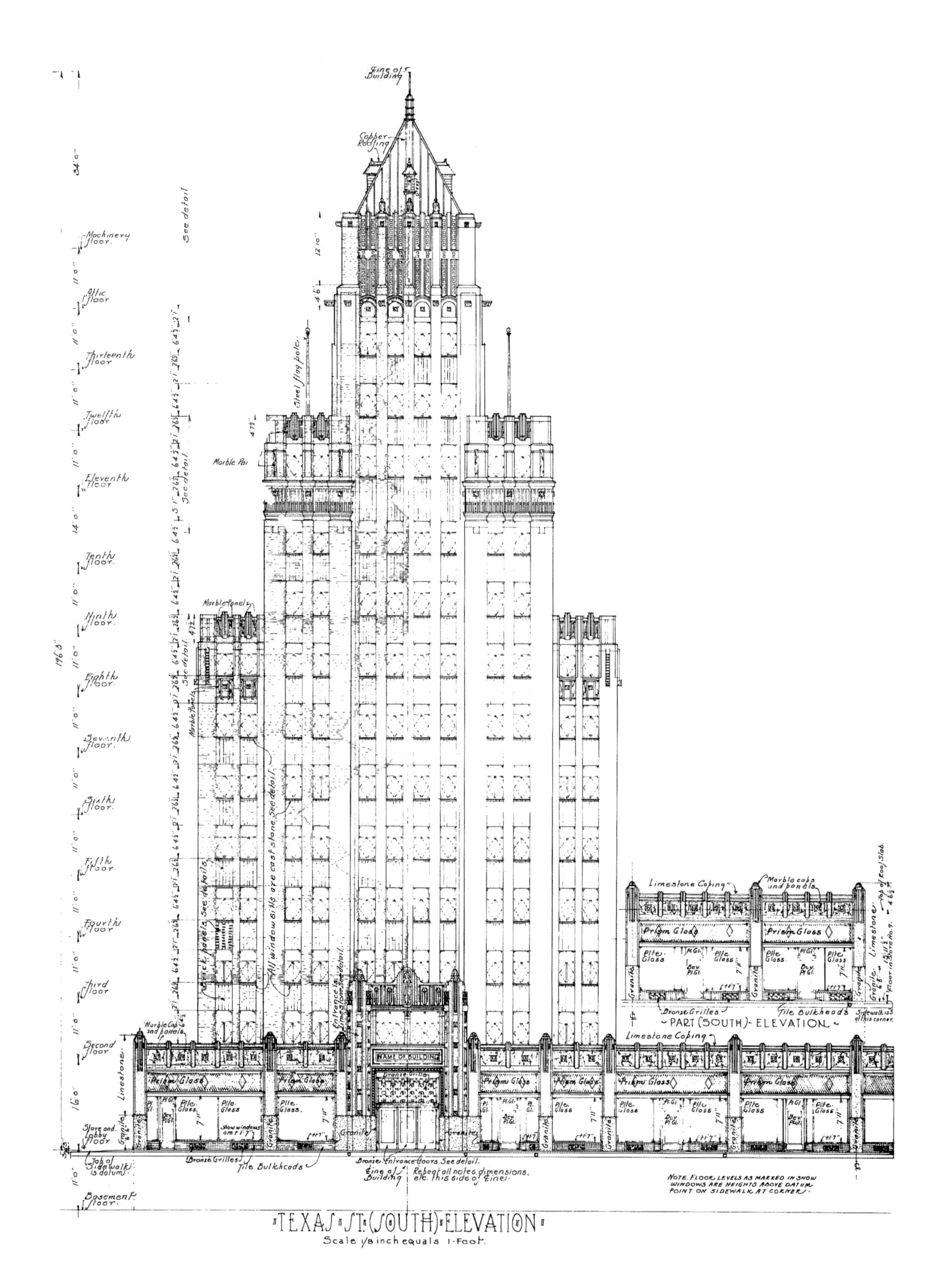
Line of Building
Copper Roofing
Steel flag pole
Marble Pan
Marble Panels
See detail
Machinery floor
Attic floor
Thirteenth floor
Twelfth floor
Eleventh floor
Tenth floor
Ninth floor
Eighth floor
Seventh floor
Sixth floor
Fifth floor
Fourth floor
Third floor
Second floor
Store and Lobby floor
Top of Sidewalk is datum
Basement floor
Brick panels. See details
All window sills are cast stone. See detail
Marble Caps and panels
Limestone
Granite
Prism Glass
Plte. Glass
Show windows are 1'-7"
NAME OF BUILDING
Bronze Grille
Bronze Grilles
Tile Bulkheads
Bronze Entrance Doors. See detail.
Line of Building
Repeat all notes, dimensions, etc. this side of Line.
Limestone Coping
Marble caps and panels
Top of Roof Slab
PART (SOUTH) ELEVATION
Sidewalk is 3' at this corner
NOTE. FLOOR LEVELS AS MARKED IN SHOW WINDOWS ARE HEIGHTS ABOVE DATUM POINT ON SIDEWALK AT CORNER.
TEXAS ST. (SOUTH) ELEVATION
Scale 1/8 inch equals 1 Foot.

the artist and architect were to start where indigenous Indian civilizations left off, we should have something here that is really of this country."[22] He also believed that ornament was inseparable from architecture, and "sources of inspiration should be geographical in the United States."[23] Bourdelle designed the bas-reliefs on the General Exhibits Building and Transportation Building, which fuse the iconography of progress with allegorical figures. Another artist contributing to the exposition, Lawrence Tenney Stevens, sculpted the allegorical statues of Texas, Spain, and the Confederacy lining the esplanade. Stevens met Dahl while both were at the American Academy in Rome.[24] It was also at the American Academy that Dahl met another artist he engaged for the exposition, Carlo Ciampaglia, a muralist who had studied at Cooper Union in New York City prior to receipt of a Prix de Rome.[25] Ciampaglia created the murals for the Transportation Building porticos, illustrating the progression of technology affecting modes of travel and mechanical devices for transportation and agriculture. In the forty-foot niche at the entrance of the Administration Building, he painted the mural depicting the state's resources behind the allegorical figure *The Spirit of the Centennial.*

Dahl relied on Juan B. Larrinaga, a set designer in Hollywood, to contribute an authentically Mexican and Mesoamerican design. Additionally, Larrinaga had previous experience working with exposition architecture, including the Panama-Pacific Exposition in San Francisco. In 1934 he was designer and art director for the California Pacific International Exposition. Larrinaga designed the ornamental bands at the parapets and surrounding dados of various buildings in Dallas Fair Park, probably contributed the color scheme, and worked as a renderer.[26] He had a reputation for producing twice the normal output in rendering, being able to accomplish two in eight hours.[27] In a profile of Larrinaga, the author claimed "The Texas Centennial Exposition building program will set a new style which is destined to have a lasting effect upon the future architecture of the world."[28]

Dahl explained that Texanic style was "strong and bold, a quality possessed to an unusual degree by the majority of the residents of Texas."[29] The national status conferred by this monumental project (the largest memorial at the time was the exposition's Hall of State, in the largest state in the continental United States) culminated on June 12, 1937, when President Franklin Delano Roosevelt attended Centennial festivities.

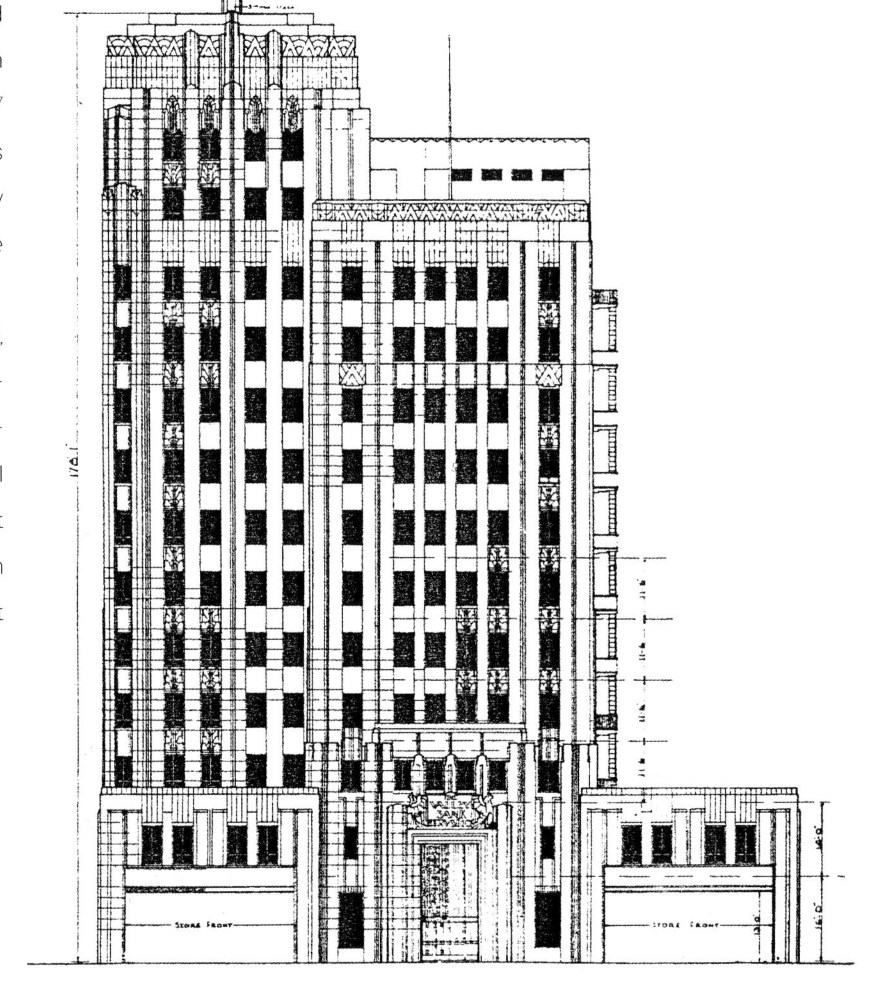

Valley Bank and Trust Company Building, Phoenix, Arizona, 1929, Morgan, Walls, and Clements, architects, in association with H. H. Green, main elevation.

Opposite. Bassett Towers, 303 Texas Avenue, El Paso, 1929, Texas, Trost & Trost, architects, drawing, south elevation.

TEXAS CENTENNIAL EXPOSITION BUILDINGS

Fair Park, Dallas, Texas, 1935–36, George L. Dahl and Donald Nelson, architects;
Hall of State designed by Centennial Architects, Associated (H. B. Thomason; Dewitt & Washburn; Fooshee & Cheek; Walter P. Sharp; Ralph Bryan; Anton Korn; Mark Lemmon; Flint & Brass; T. J. Galbraith; Arthur Thomas; Donald Barthelme of Houston; Adams & Adams of San Antonio).

The park plan and renderings were published in *Pencil Points*, February 1936. George Dahl was assisted by Juan B. Larrinaga, artist and colorist from California, who had worked on the San Francisco and San Diego expositions. Donald Nelson had contributed to Chicago's Century of Progress Exposition. Dahl was a pioneer in fast-track design, which allowed construction to begin before the final designs were finished for the Centennial buildings. The Centennial was the first exposition to be air-conditioned. Unlike previous exposition architecture, Dahl conceived these buildings as permanent, and he personally designed the Administration Building, Hall of Varied Industries, Hall of Transportation, Hall of United States, Hall of Foods, and Museum of Natural History. Fair Park cost $25 million and employed numerous people, a significant accomplishment during the Depression. Eight buildings were erected by the Exposition Commission, two by the federal government, and one by the state of Texas, The Hall of State, which cost $1.3 million and was the most expensive building in Texas at the time.

1

1. Entrance to Dallas Fair Park.

2. The United States Building featured bas-reliefs by Julian Garnsey at the base.

3. Raoul Jossett's large-scale sculpture on the Administration Building is designated the Spirit of the Centennial; the mural is the work of Carlo Ciampaglia. The Bluebonnet Girl, Frances Nalle, was selected by the artists to represent the Texas Centennial Exposition, and Jossett used her as a model when sculpting *Spirit of the Centennial*.

2

3

1836
936

4

5

6

4. Rendering of color scheme. George Dahl and Donald Nelson were assisted by Juan B. Larrinaga. Dallas Historical Society, Texas Centennial Exposition Archives.

5. Pavilion of Transportation Building, designed by Dahl, with sculpture by Lawrence Tenney Stevens. The buildings were illustrated in *The Architect & Engineer*, February 1936. Stevens created the allegorical statues of Texas, Spain, and the Confederacy appearing in front of the three pavilions of the Transportation Building.

6. Detail of *Locomotive*; a Caddo Indian and an eagle symbolize this mode of transportation, one of Pierre Bourdelle's cameo relief panels on the Transportation Building. Bourdelle was well known for his murals in Union Terminal in Cincinnati, Ohio.

7. The monumental scale of the Centennial Buildings is evident in the east entrance portico to the Transportation Building; the mural was painted by Carlo Ciampaglia.

8

9

10

8. Cast- and extruded-bronze entrance doors for the Hall of State.

9. Sculpture above the entrance to the Hall of State, *Tejas Warrior*, is the work of Allie V. Tennant.

10. The Hall of State's central pavilion is flanked by symmetrical wings with porticos. *Southern Architectural Review*, December 1936, discussed the decoration of the Hall of State in great detail.

11. Detail of colored cement pylons with cavo-relievo by Bourdelle define the reflection pool running the length of the Esplanade of State, and the Hall of State in the background.

12

12. Hall of State. The interior of the Great Hall of Texas is 90 feet long, 50 feet high, and 65 feet wide. Murals illustrating the history of the state are by Eugene Savage, who was assisted by four Texas artists: James Buchanan Winn, Revean Bassett, William Smith, and Lonnie Lyon. The murals were considered to be the largest in the world at the time.

13

14

15

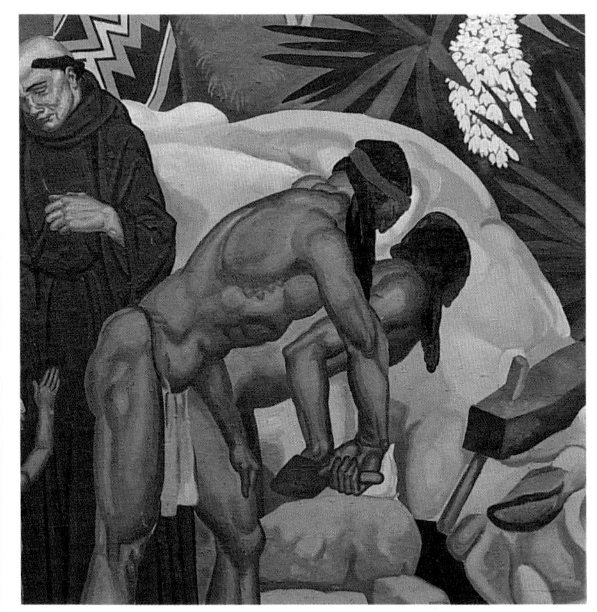

16

13. The Great Hall's dado is Belgian black marble. Six "Thrones of State" still have original upholstery, and were designed by Adams & Adams. Columns in the Great Hall are Texas limestone, filled with marine fossils. Detail of north wall.

14. Great Hall. Joseph C. Renier designed the gold medallion bas-relief. Donald Barthelme originally conceived of this terminus for the hall as a huge stone carved with events from Texas history. Gutzon Borglum was consulted regarding this concept, but Barthelme and he were unable to resolve differences: and their encounter was so acrimonious that for the remainder of the project architects were not allowed to communicate with artists directly.

15. Great Hall, detail of mural on north wall.

16. Hall of State's semicircular pavilion, the Hall of Heroes, contains six eight-foot-high bronze statues by Pompeo Copini of Texas's most illustrious men.

TEXAS & PACIFIC RAILROAD PASSENGER TERMINAL AND WAREHOUSE

1600 Throckmorton Avenue, Fort Worth, Texas, 1931, Herman Paul Koeppe of Wyatt C. Hedrick, architect.

The building incorporates an office tower above the station. The station and office tower have separate entrances. A limestone course is limited to the first three floors, above a base of pink marble. The blond brick is typically used in Texas. The warehouse is a vast space allowing tenants to store, refrigerate, and distribute merchandise or commodities which have been or need to be shipped on the railroad. Even the warehouse is embellished with limestone window headers and tile bands on the buff brick building.

1. A cast-aluminum marquee protects the passenger terminal entrance, which is separate from that used by the office-tower tenants.

2. General view of terminal.

2

1

3

3. Detail of marquee over office-tower entrance.

4. A band composed of stepped diamonds and raised brick chevrons appears above the ware-house's loading docks. Despite the warehouse's size, 8 stories high and 611 feet by 100 feet, the piers and ornament modulate the mass.

5. Bays and parapet of the warehouse.

6. The interior of the passenger terminal is encrusted with gilded and enameled molded-plaster ornament. Bronze ventilation grilles flank the entrance to the concourse.

4

5

6

WRMC

WILL ROGERS MEMORIAL AUDITORIUM

3301 West Lancaster Avenue, Fort Worth, Texas, 1934–36, Wyatt C. Hedrick & Elmer G. Withers, architects.

2

The auditorium is reinforced concrete and steel with masonry walls of brick. Designed to accommodate music, theater, a convention hall, and a coliseum for horse shows and rodeos, the complex was illustrated in *The American City,* May 1939. Design and supervision were attributed to Withers in this publication, although the design details are generally attributed to Herman Koeppe, chief designer at Hedrick's firm. At 208 feet high, Pioneer Tower was a highly visible landmark during the 1930s.

1. General view.

2. Bronco rider sculpture on east elevation of coliseum.

3

4

5

6

3. The lobby is austerely decorated with a band of stenciled motifs on the ceiling and column capitals and terrazzo floor.

4. Detail of mural frieze, which recounts the history of Fort Worth, from the original native inhabitants to cow town and, finally, to modern city. Designed by Koeppe, the tiles for this WPA project were produced by Mosaic Tile Company of Zanesville, Ohio.

5. Gates surrounding entrance.

6. Door surrounds are Texas shell stone with aluminum keystone ornament.

7. Central portion of tile frieze.

S. H. KRESS

El Paso, Oregon and Mills Streets, El Paso, Texas, 1937, Edward H. Sibbert, architect.

2

Edward H. Sibbert was the architect for the Samuel H. Kress Company from 1929 to 1954. El Paso Kress was one of Sibbert's two favorite stores (the other being the New York Kress on 5th Avenue, which has been demolished). The Oregon Street elevation differs from the north (Mills Street) and the east (Mesa Avenue) elevations. Clad with pale beige terra-cotta, produced by the Cladding & McBean Company in California, who supplied the product for all Kress stores constructed west of the Mississippi, the details were modeled by Sibbert, who rarely relied on stock mold patterns for ornament.

1. The mechanical tower on the corner of Mills and Oregon Streets is concealed by polychrome terra-cotta latticed tiles resembling a *mirador*, a screened, often elevated space where Islamic women could view the street without being seen. Sibbert has synthesized decorative elements derived from the Alhambra in Spain.

2. Oregon Street elevation.

3. Three bays form the Mesa Avenue elevation, terminating in polychrome terra-cotta keystones and finials. A cornice band is composed of imbricated arches.

4. Detail of parapet and finials display qualities found in Islamic architecture.

1

3

4

SHAFFER HOTEL

103 East Main Street, Mountainair, New Mexico, 1925–40, Clem "Pop" Shaffer, designer.

1

2

3

4 5

The Shaffer is a simple two-story hotel embellished with incised concrete motifs derived from Navajo culture, such as the inverted swastika, a directional symbol. Once the destination of tourists, the hotel featured various "creatures" in stone set in concrete stiles on fences around the hotel, reminiscent of Zuni animal fetishes.

Nearby Rancho Bonito consists of various small log and stone houses and a large barn where Shaffer worked, also heavily embellished with his carved figures and other motifs.

1. Fence detail.

2. Interior of café located in the hotel, with window transom and curtain rod carved by Shaffer.

3. Façade.

4. The ceiling of the hotel café is elaborately painted with Thunderbird motifs and geometric ornamentation derived from Native American culture.

5. Detail of opalescent glass windows in the hotel café and carved cornice molding.

KIMO THEATER

Central Avenue at Fifth Street SW, Albuquerque, New Mexico, 1926–27, Carl Boller and Robert Boller, architects.

The KiMo was conceived by Italian immigrant Oreste Bachechi as an homage to the Pueblos and other Native Americans; the name was provided by Pablo Abeita, governor of Isleta Pueblo, and means "king of its kind."

1. Walls of the mezzanine are painted by Carl von Hassler to portray the various "Seven Cities of Cibola," a mythical quest of the Spanish conquistadors. Cast-plaster steer skulls are painted with glazed enamel and provide the illumination on the mezzanine and in the theater.

2. General view.

3. Determined to build "America's Foremost Indian Theater," Bachechi instructed Carl Boller and muralist von Hassler to travel around New Mexico to immerse themselves in the cultures and architectural styles of the Southwest. The resulting structure synthesizes their experiences. Wrought-aluminum door handles are in the shape of Kachinas. Pueblo deities and prehistoric murals inspired the painted corbels and ceiling of the foyer.

4. Detail of skulls, which refer to the Buffalo Dance performed at Taos Pueblo every January. Inez B. Westlake worked on the interior design; she had previously worked with Trost & Trost on the Hotel Franciscan.

2

3

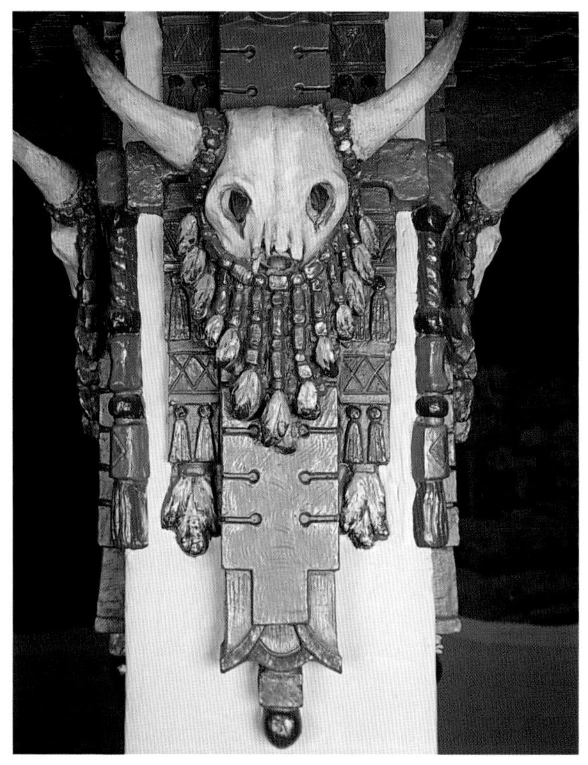

4

5

5. Polychrome terra-cotta shields alternating with spindles form a band across the façade. Shields correspond to piers and cascade down in diminishing steps, composed of triangles, chevrons, and stylized feathers in a manner of the *faldoncito* of Mexican baroque architecture. Shields decorated with feathers and other appendages were often carried by participants in Indian ceremonial parades during the 1920s.

6. Rendering by Carl Boller of the KiMo Theater, without signage as the rendering was made prior to the naming; rendering courtesy of Oreste Bachechi.

7. Detail of tile in the foyer.

8. Polychrome terra-cotta capital composed of opposing frets embellishes the stucco pier, flanking the KiMo Theater's marquee.

6

BACHECHI'S·THEATRE·ALBVQVERQVE·N·M·-BOLLER·BROTHERS·ARCHITECTS·LOS ANGELES·CAL·&·KANSAS CITY·MO·

7

8

ALBUQUERQUE INDIAN HOSPITAL

(Public Health Service Indian Hospital). 801 Vassar Drive NE, Albuquerque, New Mexico, 1934, Hans Stamm, architect.

The Albuquerque Indian Hospital was originally built as a tuberculosis sanitarium, and was the first building to be constructed by the Bureau of Indian Affairs deviating from a standard design. Stepped keystones, corbeled arches, and the linoleum floor inlaid with the profile of a Navajo are specific to the Southwest.

2

1. Hans Stamm, chief of the Architectural Group of the Bureau of Indian Affairs, was directed to consider the region's built environment. Traditional Pueblo architecture has been transformed into a modernistic building complex with stepped parapets and turquoise-green terra-cotta coping. A T-shaped structure, the hospital is terraced in shallow tiers and steps.

2. North wing.

3. Detail of stucco resembling an adobe surface; terra-cotta piers.

4. The color scheme of the interior lobby suggests Stamm may have seen Navajo rugs woven in the Tec Nos Pas region, where the weavers had been encouraged to return to native dyes such as mistletoe, which produces a soft mustard, and indigo, which produces a range of blues.

1 3

4

MARICOPA COUNTY COURTHOUSE AND PHOENIX CITY BUILDING

125 West Washington Street, Phoenix, Arizona, 1928, Edward Neild, architect of building; Lescher & Mahoney, architects for Phoenix City entrance.

1

Illustrated in *Architecture*, October 1931, the Maricopa County Courthouse and Phoenix City Building bear a similarity in form to another Edward Neild courthouse— Caddo Parish Courthouse in Shreveport, Louisiana.

1. General view.

2. Courthouse entrance on the north elevation, flanked by cast-iron light fixtures terminating in thunderbird finials and pink granite piers.

2

MARICOPA COVNTY
COVRT HOVSE
125 W. WASHINGTON
NO WEAPONS
NO WEAPONS

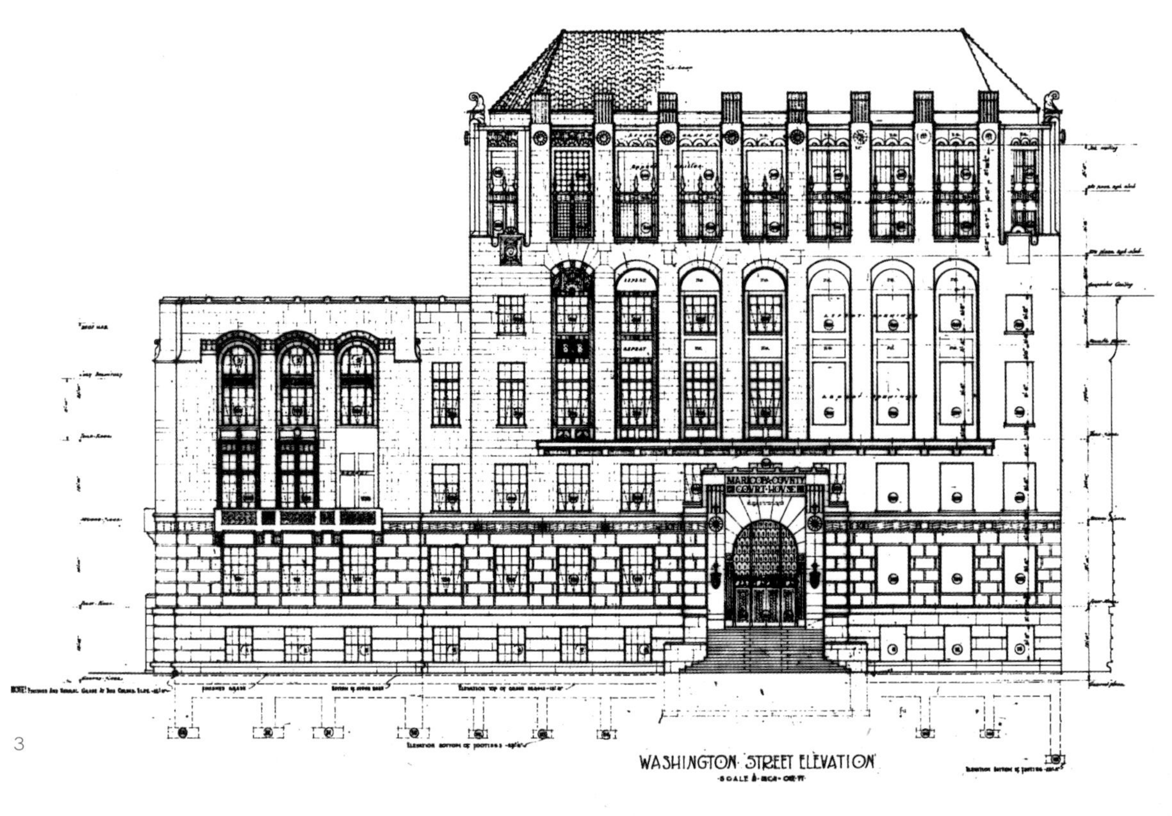

3

3. Washington Street elevation drawing of Maricopa County Courthouse Phoenix City Hall, Facilities Management, Maricopa County.

4. Volute pier cap and wrought-iron Thunderbird detail of light fixtures on the courthouse entrance.

5. Polychrome terra-cotta ornament surrounds the windows.

6. Volute pier caps with stylized sunflowers at the parapet.

4

5

ARIZONA BILTMORE HOTEL

Twenty-fourth Avenue at Missouri Street, Phoenix, Arizona, 1929. Albert Chase McArthur, architect.

1

2

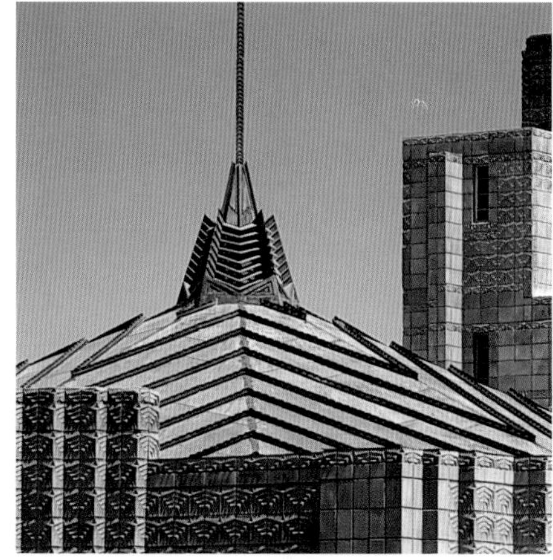

3

4

The Arizona Biltmore was illustrated in *Architectural Record,* July 1929. Using a textile block similar to Frank Lloyd Wright's, with whom Albert Chase McArthur apprenticed, the pattern is derived from McArthur's theosophical ideas and a theory that sound can be visualized.

1. General view.

2. Patinated copper roof of ballroom.

3. Projecting eaves are pierced.

4. Rendering by McArthur of forecourt and entrance of Arizona Biltmore.

5. McArthur worked with Hopi sculptor Emry Kopta to design the modular, rectangular concrete blocks. Concrete and glass were molded and a three-coordinate system was used for construction.

Gough
1895

CALIFORNIA AND THE PACIFIC NORTHWEST

California exhuded the aura of paradise by virtue of its natural environment. Jasmine and orange blossoms proliferated; sunshine appeared virtually every day. Date palm orchards extended into the desert, and miles of wide sandy beaches were strung along the coast. Such an abundant ambiance invited migration (although many wealthy Americans merely wintered in Pasadena and San Diego), and early in the twentieth century there was also a viable industry which could provide employment—film. The realm of movies was everything the natural environment was not—artificial, manipulated, a world of chimera. Motifs from these opposing spheres characterize art deco architecture in California. The other major influence on design was transportation. Long Beach was a vital seaport, diverse types of aircraft were manufactured in Southern California, and the automobile was the primary mode of transportation.

W. Francklyn Paris, in a review of the 1925 *Exposition Internationale des Arts Décoratifs et Industriels Modernes,* stated that "Speed is not only expressed in movement, it begets a state of mind, and since curves are eloquent of repose and languor they no longer find a place in modern architecture or in the composition of surrounding objects which serve as a setting for our daily life."[1] California was devoted to design accommodating automotive traffic. Miracle Mile retailers often selected the modernistic style, with its attendant skyscraper towers, to attract customers who happened to be driving by. The style rapidly spread to the suburbs as the predominant commercial style. Reflecting the region's unique cultural and environmental heritage, imagery, such as foliation, scenes of paradise, nudes, and fruit are frequently encountered in the art deco style. The Pacific Ocean inspired motifs—seashells, crabs and fish, mermaids, and mythological figures associated with the sea, such as Neptune. The fabulous Sunset Tower Apartment Building and the Casino on Catalina Island offer fine examples of the use of regional aquatic motifs.

Pacific Avenue Apartments,
San Francisco, California, 1931,
Herman C. Baumann, architect.

Theaters have been integral to the history of California. As early as 1921, film brought modern architecture before the American public via sets for movies. Architect Joseph Urban, initially associated with the Viennese Secessionist movement in his native Austria, came to the United States in the early 1920s and became involved with William Randolph Hearst's Cosmopolitan Productions company. As art director of numerous movies for Cosmopolitan Productions, Urban merged Secessionist detail with modernist aesthetics.[2] The integration of architecture and film is illustrated by a reverse transition. Hugo Ballin, a well-known silent film director, left the industry when talking movies replaced those without sound to became an architectural muralist.

Numerous architects worked on sets in Hollywood. Juan B. Larrinaga, one of the principal designers of the Texas Centennial in 1937, while not an architect, was an innovative artist who worked as a set designer. Following college, he clerked in a department store but found the work dull and left to travel and study in Mexico.[3] Returning to California, he joined a touring opera company as interpreter and assistant to the scenic director, and from there he segued into film commissions, often movies with themes which required a knowledge of Hispanic or Mexican architecture and culture. Larrinaga was responsible for the decorative work on the sets for Douglas Fairbank's *The Gaucho* and Delores del Rio's *Carmen*.[4] In addition to design work, Larrinaga and his brother were innovators of a film technique derived from architecture, the construction of models. Filming highly detailed architectural models and miniatures allowed the cinema studios to replace expensive location work or equally expensive sets built at human scale.[5] Simultaneously, Juan Larrinaga worked on the Panama-Pacific Exposition in San Francisco, and in 1934 he was designer and art director for the California Pacific International Exposition. His contribution to Dallas Fair Park was an expression of "an architecture with the Latin-American feel of romance and golden sunshine. . . ."[6]

El Rey Theater, 5519 Wilshire Boulevard, Los Angeles, California, c. 1928, W. Cliff Balch, architect.

In California, Spanish Colonial and the Mission styles were the dominant paradigms in the early twentieth century. Many art deco theaters utilized such elements, such as El Rey on Wilshire Boulevard. Exoticism coexisted with this regionalism. In 1916 director D. W. Griffith erected a fabulous movie set for *Intolerance* on an empty lot at what is now 4473 Sunset Drive. The set was a re-creation of the ancient city of Babylon, featuring figures of elephants on hind legs atop massive fluted columns and square stepped arches. After production, the set remained standing for several years, inspiring an obsession with ziggurats and prehistoric architecture.[7] This obsession is reflected in the ziggurat on the pinnacle of the Los Angeles City Hall, built in 1926–28, and pinnacles of commercial buildings along Wilshire Boulevard. The stepped pyramidal form is equally informed by the archaeological discoveries in Mesoamerica. Robert Stacy-Judd was the primary proponent of this style, having become a convert to pre-Columbian architecture after reading John L. Stevens's *Incidents of Travel in Central America, Chiapas, and Yucatan*, published in 1841.[8] Stacy-Judd's First Baptist Church in Ventura, California, was an eloquent expression of an ancient culture woven into the fabric of the modernistic style in which the stepped pyramid was a leitmotif. Timothy Pflueger's Four Fifty Four Sutter Street Building, in San Francisco, exemplifies how Mesoamerican motifs could be manipulated within an individual modernistic vocabulary.

While Native Americans exerted tremendous influence on art deco in the Southwest, one of the few modernistic buildings in California with an overt influence is the Ahwahnee Hotel in Yosemite Village. Designed by Gilbert Stanley Underwood, a graduate of Harvard's School of Architecture and retained by Union Pacific Railways, the Ahwahnee Hotel's decorative program was influenced by native Pomo, Hupa, and Hurok basketry.[9] A Great Hall with a massive fireplace has twenty-four-foot high windows and stained glass transoms designed by Jeanette Dyer Spencer, an architect who had studied at the University of California and the École du Louvre in Paris.

When movie mogul Sid Grauman engaged the Los Angeles firm of Meyer and Holler to design the first "exotic"

el Rey

theater in Hollywood, Egypt rather than the Americas provided the inspiration. Grauman's Egyptian Theatre was highly successful and created a rage for Egyptian motifs. Encouraged by the success of the Egyptian Theatre, Meyer and Holler were next commissioned to design the famed Grauman's Chinese Theatre. With its jade-colored roofs, cinnabar terra-cotta surfaces, and gold ornamentation, Grauman's Chinese Theatre became an instant success—especially after movie stars began leaving their handprints, footprints, and signatures in the forecourt's cement (a shrewd publicity stunt that still attracts attention). Figures of dragons and other references to Chinese culture proliferate. Tickets for screenings could be purchased under an open temple structure.

Every large city on the Pacific Rim has a significant Asian population. During the 1930s Santa Fe Railroad advertisements featuring Los Angeles's Chinatown were intended to seduce tourists in search of the exotic.[10] In Chinatown merchandisers offered antiques and Asian arts avidly sought by collectors and decorators associated with the Arts and Crafts Movement, as well as by Hollywood set designers seeking inspiration.[11] K. Hope Hamilton described the influence of Chinese art on modern interiors, illustrated by the Mandarin Cafe Building in San Francisco. Hamilton considered the expression of simplicity found in Chinese arts to be appropriate to modernism. "Chinese design can only be appreciated by familiarity with motif, unit or element, which is employed with grace, symmetry and charm. Their motifs are derived from nature. . . ."[12] The original Chinatown in Los Angeles was scheduled to be demolished in order to accommodate construction of the new Union Passenger Terminal. Engineer Peter Soo Hoo worked to establish an area on north Broadway as the site for New Chinatown.[13] This was an opportunity to build in the modern idiom. Architects Erle Webster and Adrian Wilson were retained by You Chung Hong, the first Chinese American to pass the state bar exam to practice law. Hong, who was one of the primary financial developers of the project, commissioned Webster & Wilson to design the East Gate and various buildings for Los Angeles's New Chinatown.[14]

Elks Building (Park Plaza Hotel), 607 South Park View Street, Los Angeles, California, 1924, Claude Beelman, architect, with William Curlett.

By the early 1920s, the film industry had replaced oil, shipping, and agriculture as Los Angeles's leading industry. To control distribution, companies such as RKO, Twentieth Century-Fox, and Warner Brothers began to lease or build movie theaters such as Warner Brothers's Western Theater, now the Wiltern Theater. By the late 1920s, issues of cost had begun to pervade theater design.[15] In 1925, theater construction cost anywhere from $125 to $200 per seat. The modernistic style, with its geometric features, was less expensive than other ornate decorative styles and, consequently, frequently selected for theater design. Due to the proliferation of theater construction and competition, the Western Theater closed after only one year in operation. This fabulous concoction, the result of Stiles O. Clements's collaboration with C. Albert Lansburgh, noted theater architect, exuded luxury; it was a magical realm adorned with sun and wave motifs and tropical foliation. The sun appears in plaster relief on the marquee's ceiling, over the corbeled arches of the lobby, and on the auditorium ceiling. The original furniture was designed by Kem Weber. Despite its initial failure, the theater reopened in the mid-1930s and operated continuously until 1979. Fortunately, the Wiltern Theater (along with the adjacent Pellissier Building) was rescued from demolition by the concerted efforts of local preservationists and restored in the early 1980s.

Los Angeles was becoming a major American city, and a new city hall reflecting this status was designed by John C. Austin, John and Donald Parkinson, Albert C. Martin, and Austin Whittlesey, Associated Architects. The plans were approved in 1923. As a municipal entity, City Hall was exempt from the 150-foot height restriction, and consequently it became the tallest building in the city. It has a theatrical profile, with a stepped pyramid at its pinnacle. The remainder of the building is a mélange of streamlined neoclassical and Spanish Colonial elements, with various visual references to local history, a trait frequently evident in public buildings as a result of the Nebraska State Capitol. John Austin wrote, "the architects [were] determined not to confine themselves to any particular design."[16] The ornament

on the bronze doors, he went on to explain, depicts many "notable events in connection with the early history and settlement of Southern California, particularly, of Los Angeles."[17] When completed in 1928, Los Angeles City Hall ushered in a new era of civic construction in Southern California.

Not only were civic amenities increasing, but California was where the American dream of owning a single-family dwelling could be realized. Houses built during the 1920s and 1930s continued to be the conservative revival styles, Mediterranean, Spanish Colonial, Tudor, and French Provincial, despite the visibility and promotion of modernistic work such as Frank Lloyd Wright's. Modernistic design of apartment buildings erected during this period reflected twentieth-century amenities. The December 1930 issue of *The Architect and Engineer* was devoted to apartment houses. Albert H. Larsen, the architect of numerous apartment buildings in San Francisco, described the financing process: "[The architect] must know real estate values, rental locations in the city for various types of tenants, building costs, financing costs and methods, and operating costs. The preliminary design of an apartment therefore should be done by the typewriter."[18] "We find the average apartment building of today equipped with electrical refrigerators, electric ranges, electric ventilated kitchens, some have electric dishwashers, built-in bottle and can openers, radio systems, cedar chests, built-in drawers, shoe racks, cellarette closets and whatnot—with numberless other all new devices continually placed on the market and offered by speculative builders to attract possible buyers or tenants."[19]

Lloyd Wright, Frank Lloyd Wright's son, demonstrated his ability to combine strong volumes with intricate massing and austere ornament. By 1923, when he designed the Taggart house, Lloyd Wright had mastered an organic approach to architecture. While supervising the construction of his father's textile-block houses, he gained a superior technical understanding of that material. By the late 1920s, Lloyd Wright was designing such masterpieces as the 1926–28 Samuel-Navarro house (unfortunately remodeled) and the Derby house, with its underground garage so integrated into the design that it appears to support the house above. A garage was de rigueur in the design program for California houses of the 1920s and 1930s. A member of the Department of Commerce's Division of Building and Housing remarked in 1929 that "the automobile, besides permitting residences to spread out to suburban areas served by private cars . . . has affected the size, shape and features of the lot and of the house."[20] So too did the ever-expanding bathroom. Inspired by their glamorous counterparts in movies, bathrooms in Los Angeles homes became larger and more sybaritic than ever before. Not only the center of celluloid, endless suburbs in Southern California provided the primary component of the American dream—a house and two-car garage.

United States Post Office,
Hollywood Branch,
1615 Wilcox Avenue,
Los Angeles, California, 1937,
Claude Beelman, architect.

The coastline north of Los Angeles becomes wilder and rougher, and beyond San Francisco, the Pacific Northwest becomes a distinct region. Mount Rainier dominates Seattle's landscape, and suggested the concept of gradation of color to the architect A. H. Albertson for the Northern Life Tower.[21] Originally, the Northwest was inhabited by sophisticated cultures such as the Haida, Kwakiutl, and Tlingit tribes, associated with potlatches, brilliantly painted wooden masks, and totem poles. Inland, between the Rocky Mountains and the Cascade Range, the Plateau Indians, including the Flathead, Nez Percé, and Spokane tribes, among others, used their hunting skill to supply furs to British, French, and Russian traders prior to American acquisition. Modernistic architecture in the Pacific Northwest rarely contained overt references to these native inhabitants, however. The tunnel entrance to the 1940 Murrow Bridge in Seattle, designed by Lloyd Lovegren with James Fitzgerald as sculptor, is an exception.

Northern Life Tower is an expression of the extraordinary landscape surrounding Seattle. Designed by Albertson with Joseph W. Wilson and Paul Richardson, Associates, its frontage consumes half a block on Third Avenue in Seattle's central business district overlooking Puget Sound. The tower's brick and terra-cotta was produced by Gladding, McBean & Company's northwestern plant in colors of dark heather brown at the base, which becomes lighter as

Right. Oregon State Capitol Building, 900 Court Street NE, Salem, Oregon, 1936–39, Francis Keally and George Jacoby of Trowbridge & Livingston, 900 Court Street NE, Salem, Oregon. The capitol building was the result of a national competition. "The Pioneer," sculpted and cast by Ulric H. Ellerhusen in his New Jersey studio, is a twenty-two-foot bronze with gold leaf statue on the pinnacle of white Vermont marble.

the height increases, culminating in a pale buff.[22] "Mt. Rainier, the greatest neighboring landmark, is always white at the top with perpetual snow and grades in strength of color downward into the deep evergreen of the forests below."[23] The building was "the endeavor to express the meaning of solidity, durability and power by assuming the building to be hewn out of the solid block with nothing overhanging, everything smooth, ornament flat and incised. . . . The building was conceived as rising out of the ground, not as sitting traditionally upon the surface—as a part of earth rather than a thing apart from it."[24] At night, Northern Life Tower was illuminated, "simulating the phantasmagoric play of the Northern Lights."[25] Attracted by the explosive growth occurring in the city, Albertson, who graduated from Columbia University in New York City, moved to Seattle in 1907.

Typically, architects were often raised and educated on the East Coast and, realizing that Seattle was a growing city, moved there to practice independently. Carl F. Gould was born into a prestigious New Jersey family, traveled widely, attended Phillips Exeter Academy, and graduated from Harvard prior to attending the *École des Beaux-Arts* in Paris from 1898 to 1903. When he returned to New York City, he worked for McKim, Mead & White and several other firms, but without great success. Via working with George B. Post, he associated with Daniel H. Burnham, who was working on the San Francisco City Plan.[26] Realizing that there were greater opportunities in Seattle, Gould relocated there and practiced with Charles H. Bebb. Gould was responsible for creating the University of Washington's architecture department, and the firm designed various buildings on its campus. Bebb & Gould was a major firm during the 1920s through the 1930s, until Gould's premature death. Although the *Beaux-Arts* clearly exerted an influence early in his career, Bebb began working within the modern idiom by the late 1920s, although very little of his work was purely art deco. Expressing the technology of telecommunications, Bebb & Gould relied on modernistic ornament for several Pacific Telephone & Telegraph buildings. One of the most distinctly deco buildings was the result of his collaboration with John Graham, Sr., designing the United States Marine Hospital in Seattle. Apparently, when the initial design was submitted to the Treasury Department, it was not approved. It was discreetly suggested to the architects that aluminum should be substituted for the metal originally specified, and when the architects made that correction, the project was approved.[27] Gould, who was the chief designer of Bebb & Gould, became increasingly modern by 1930. This process is extremely well documented in his working drawings and sketches for the Seattle Art Museum. Originally neoclassical, the museum was transmogrified throughout the design process into a sleek Moderne building with an art deco grille above the entrance.[28]

Bon Marché was found in 1890 by Edward Nordhoff, who had worked as a delivery boy in Paris before emigrating to the United States, where he worked as a floor walker in Marshall Field and Company prior to moving to Seattle for his health.[29] Nordhoff's memories of a shop in Paris with a plaque to greet customers influenced the name

Opposite. Shell Building, 100 Bush Street, San Francisco, California, 1929–30, George W. Kelham, architect. The structure was illustrated in *The Architect & Engineer*, July 1930. The company's logo appears on the bronze transom grille.

of the dry goods emporium he opened in Seattle. His wife learned Chinook, an Indian language used by traders for centuries, so that she could communicate with indigenous patrons.[30] The emporium made Nordhoff's fortune when he was the first to bring pennies into circulation in Seattle, introducing the 69-cent and 89-cent sales in the 1890s. The Klondike gold rush was a major influence on the expansion of Seattle's economy. Voyagers often outfitted themselves and purchased supplies in Seattle, marketed as the "Gateway to Alaska," before leaving for the Klondike.[31] Bon Marché continued to expand, successively building larger stores until culminating in the 1929 store designed by John Graham, Sr., another major Seattle architect. Bon Marché was progressive in its support of regional industries; knitting and textile mills, furniture and clothing factories, benefitted from the merchandiser's policy of buying and selling local products.[32] This commitment to local industry was manifested in the 1929 building, which contained lighting fixtures and furniture produced locally. "Every structural unit of The Bon Marché which could be procured in the Pacific Northwest was bought there."[33]

Considered to be "The Gateway to the Orient" as well as to Alaska, Seattle was the appropriate site for the con-

Color pencil sketch on trace by Carl Gould, one of the numerous studies he made in the process of designing the Seattle Art Museum. MSCUA, University of Washington Libraries, UW13337.

struction of a movie palace inspired by Chinese architecture.[34] The 1926 5th Avenue Theatre is situated within the Italian Renaissance revival Skinner Building and both were designed by architect Robert C. Reamer. The authenticity of the theater was due to Gustav Liljestrom, who was trained in China before moving to San Francisco, where he became chief designer at S & G Gump Company of San Francisco. Liljestrom imported the textiles and furniture decorating the theater. "Consummate care was taken in the veracity of its design, the walls, the carvings, the sculpture, the paintings, the coloring, the fixtures, the hangings, the floor coverings, the objets d'art and minute decorative details finding their inspiration in China's most cherished institutions."[35] Suspended above the auditorium, the dome of the theater is derived from the Throne Room of the Imperial Palace in Beijing. "Coiled in an azure sphere and surrounded by glowing hues of cloud-red, emblematic of calamity and warfare; blue, of Great Dragon, guardian of the heavens and foe of evil spirits."[36] The remainder of the theater is an extravagant mélange of the Summer Palace, the Temple of Heavenly Peace, and the Throne Room at the Imperial Palace in Beijing.

Chinese culture may have seemed exotic and foreign, yet these immigrants were integral to the development of the West. Responsible for incredible feats involving fearlessness and endurance, the Transcontinental Railroad could not have been constructed without these tireless workers who were committed to surviving in America. Alien but citizens, a position similar to Native Americans, these cultures provided design inspiration for the Jazz Age. New cities arose in California and the Pacific Northwest during the late nineteenth century. Rapid expansion occurred in the early part of the following century, producing wonderful examples of art deco architecture. The architects were inspired by magnificent landscapes, cultures which were part of America yet exotic, and regional industries which defined the twentieth century.

Bottom left. Pencil rendering of Northern Life lobby, reproduced in their inaugural brochure. MSCUA, University of Washington Libraries.

Bottom right. Bon Marché, 1929. John Graham Sr., architect. Illustration by Ernest R. Norling, for *The Bon Marché* (Seattle: Western Printing Company, 1929). MSCUA, University of Washington Libraries.

GRAUMAN'S CHINESE THEATRE

6925 Hollywood Boulevard, Los Angeles, California, 1927, Meyer & Holler, architects.

1

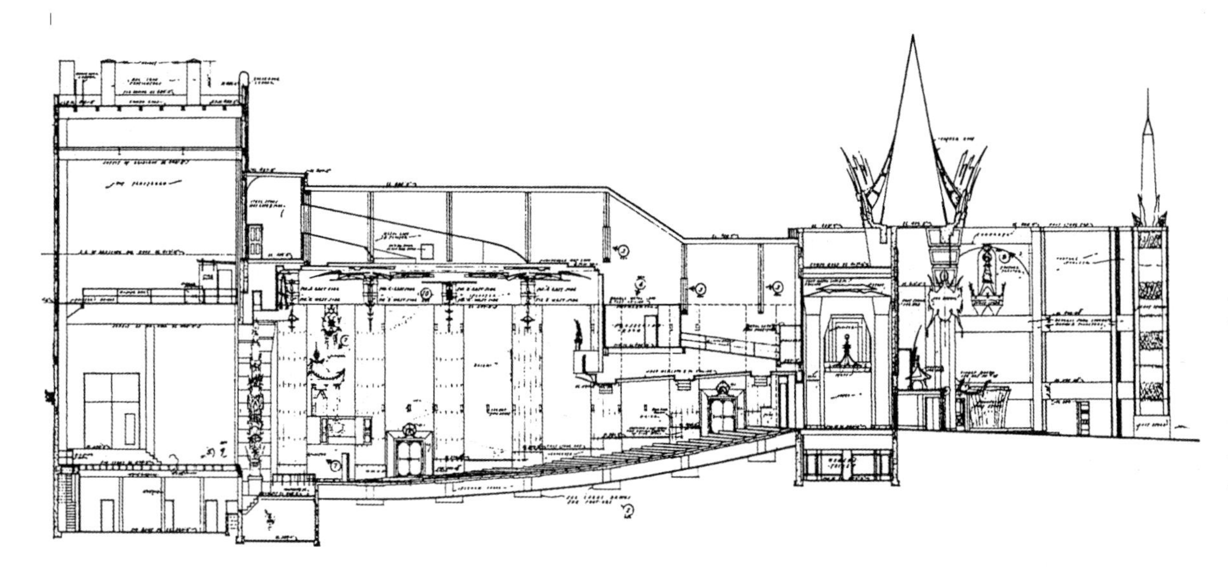

Grauman's Chinese Theatre was built by movie mogul Sid Grauman, who introduced the concept of "exotic" theaters. The August 20, 1927, edition of *American Architect* included two major articles regarding the project accompanied by photographs and drawings of the theater.

1. Elevation drawing, *The Architectural Record*, August 1927.

2. *Chi shou*, or animal figures, which on the Grauman Theatre are tiny bronze dragons, run along the edges of the pagoda roofs. The green verdigris copper symbolized jade.

3. The forecourt and ticket booth comprise a temple structure, which incorporates actual building techniques from Chinese architecture, such as wood-beam framing, *chia liang*. Greek revival elements appear in the use of stylized capitals and a running fret motif. The dragon relief was modeled from a stone slab, thirty feet high.

2

3

6925

MAUSOLEUM OF THE GOLDEN WEST

4201 East Whittier Boulevard, Los Angeles, California, 1927, Ross Montgomery, architect.

1

2

3

4

The Mausoleum, located at the New Calvary Cemetery, consists of multiple domes and arcades, constructed of reinforced concrete with color stucco plaster. Montgomery employed cast-concrete grilles as a means of reducing the building's weight as well as creating a sense of the balmy climate of California.

1. Polychrome cast-concrete domes and details.

2. Family vaults are placed in the flanking pavilions facing the entrance court.

3. Murals in the entrance.

4. Family chapels, such as the Mauer chapel, are embellished with brass grilles and stained glass.

5. The Mausoleum features a ziggurat, a popular form during the 1920s, which gained national attention when the Los Angeles City Hall was built. Acanthus leaves ornament the parapet.

5

OVIATT BUILDING & PENTHOUSE

617 South Olive Street, Los Angeles, California, 1927–28, Albert Walker & Percy A. Eisen, architects.

1

The Oviatt is an office tower and ground-floor commercial space, built for a haberdashery, Alexander & Oviatt. James Oviatt resided in the penthouse on the twelfth floor. Carl Jules Weyl, who was employed by Walker & Eisen in the mid-1920s, also played an important role in the design. The plein air lobby of the building, illustrated in *Architecture,* May 1930, and *California Arts & Architecture,* February 1929, has Benedict nickel (nickel silver) mailbox and elevator doors with panels of Lalique glass, executed by A. J. Bayer Co., an ornamental iron and bronze company in Los Angeles. Thirty tons of glass were shipped from Paris for this commission.

1. Pinnacle of tower with cast-iron finial.

2. The penthouse opens onto a large terrace; steps lead to the tower.

2

3. James Oviatt had attended the Paris Exposition Internationale des Arts Décoratifs et Industriels Modernes in 1925 and, enthused by the style, commissioned René Lalique to provide decorative glass for the Oviatt Building. The bathroom is intact; walls are incised and glazed plaster. The metalwork is maillechort, an alloy of nickel, zinc, and copper. A steam room is tiled in yellow. Oviatt's commission was the first commercial and largest single commission for Lalique, who designed lamps, windows, sconces, and even display cases. The bathroom windows are sandblasted and etched.

5

4

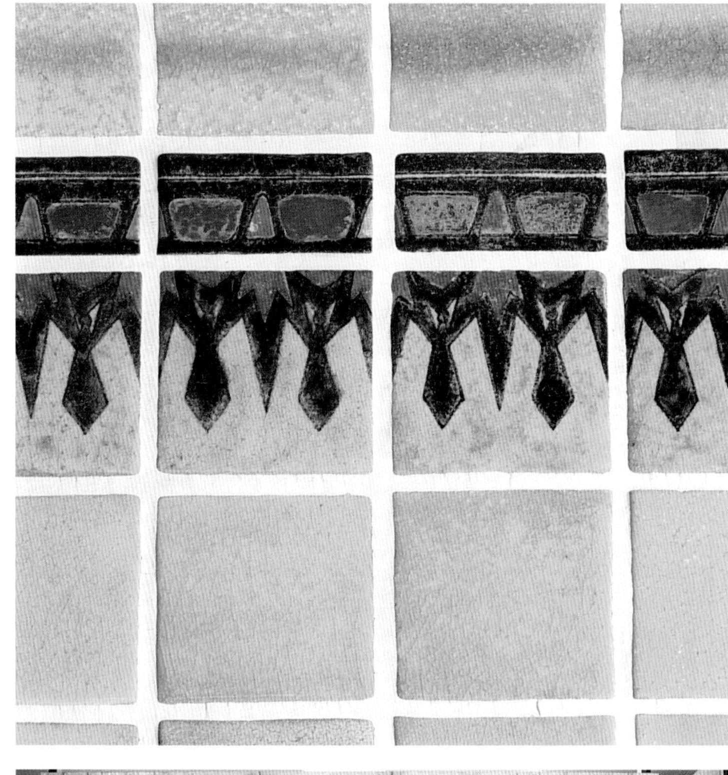

6

4. Detail of tile in the steam room.

5. Bathroom counter is Moroccan flamme marble.

6. Maillechort fireplace screen.

7. Original library in the penthouse.

7

SBORA
Westmoreland
FOR LEASE
the Silk Factory

BULLOCK'S WILSHIRE DEPARTMENT STORE

3050 Wilshire Boulevard, Los Angeles, California, 1928, John & Donald Parkinson; Feil & Paradise; Jock D. Peters, architects.

2

3

Featured in *Architect & Engineer,* December 1929, and *The Architectural Record,* July 1931, the store was considered "one of the most consistently modern creations." Advertising its presence on "Miracle Mile," the tower, exceeding the permitted 150-foot building height by including a 35-foot penthouse, a 6-foot roof, and 50 feet of signage construction, is a visible beacon for automobile drivers. Jock Peters designed the interior using St. Genevieve Rose marble to contrast with neutral-tone walls, and rosewood display cases.

1. General view.

2. Detail of cast-bronze pinnacle. Bronze coping alternates with terra-cotta piers at the setbacks, materials specifically selected to reflect the California atmosphere.

3. Facing on the Bullock's Wilshire is buff terra-cotta, is faceted at the corners to produce vertical zigzags.

4. Cast-iron gates, *Time Flies,* designed by Herman Sachs, lead to the porte cochere and parking lot, effectively creating the main entrance on the back of the building, and were illustrated in *California Arts & Architecture,* January 1930.

4

1

5

5. *Speed of Transportation,* the porte cochere's ceiling mural, was created by Herman Sachs.

6. A three-part decorative light fixture features etched frosted glass.

7. *The Spirit of Sports* mural was originally designed for the sportswear shop by Gjura Stojano using thin strips of wood veneer. The walls are sycamore panels. The woodwork was executed by Vernon Fixture and Cabinet Company of Los Angeles.

8. North elevation drawing and detail of spandrels and pier caps, courtesy of The Parkinson Archives, Austin, Texas.

6

7

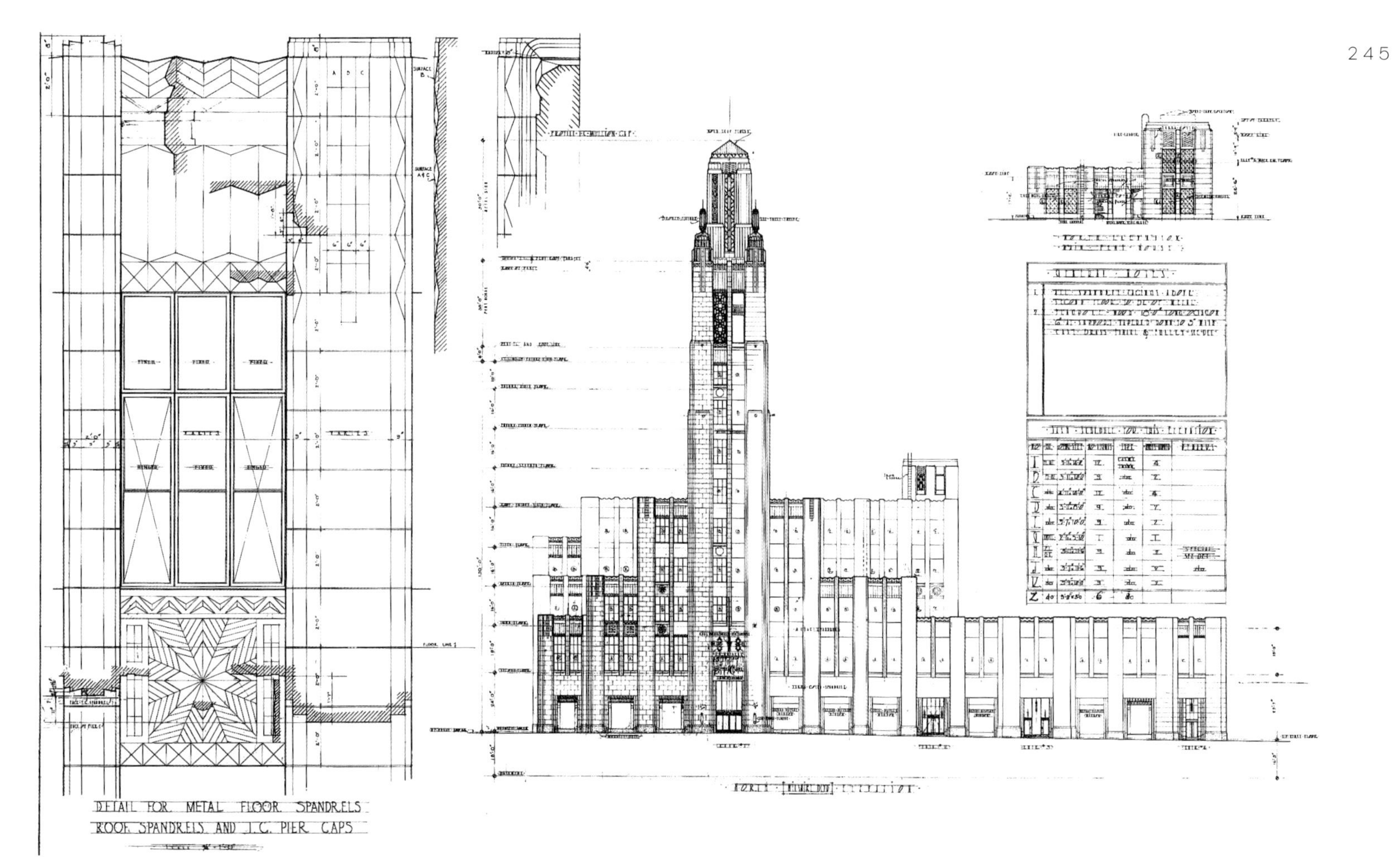
DETAIL FOR METAL FLOOR SPANDRELS
ROOF SPANDRELS AND I.C. PIER CAPS

8

B'NAI B'RITH TEMPLE

(Wilshire Boulevard Temple) 3663 Wilshire Boulevard, Los Angeles, California, 1929, Abram M. Edelman, Allison & Allison, consulting architects.

1

B'nai B'rith, consisting of a reinforced concrete shell using the cement-gun process, was designed to withstand earthquakes. The base of the auditorium is flanked by eight buttresses. The interior of the temple is an irregular octagon. Above the marble piers at the east and west walls are columns of Belgian black marble, rising thirty feet to the dome. Flanking the colonnade on each side of the auditorium are three stained glass windows designed by Oliver Smith Studios of Bryn Athyn, Pennsylvania; the six windows represent the twelve tribes of Israel. The temple was published in *The Architect & Engineer*, July 1929.

1. Detail of roof, which was originally covered with terra-cotta tile.

2. General view.

3. The Bema and Ark are walnut. The gold finish cast-bronze chandeliers, in the form of Habdalah boxes, were produced by the Meyberg Company of Los Angeles. The two menorah lights were also designed by Meyberg. Walnut wainscoting encircles the interior. Vern O. Knudsen of the University of California at Los Angeles provided the research to produce perfect acoustical conditions.

2

3

4

5

4. Detail of mural in lunette on the east wall of the auditorium. Funded by a generous donation from the Warner brothers, the murals were painted by Hugo Ballin.

5. The community room in the temple's basement is ornately decorated, including Meyberg chandeliers and a stucco cornice.

6. Detail of Smith's windows, the mural, and capitals inspired by Oriental motifs.

7. Detail of mural.

6

WARNER BROTHERS WESTERN THEATER & PELLISIER BUILDING

(Wiltern Theater). 3790 Wilshire Boulevard, Los Angeles, California, 1930–31, Morgan, Walls & Clements, architects.

1

The theater was developed in the district known at the time as Uptown L.A. by Henry de Roulet, the grandson of the owners (Germain and Marie Julie Pellisier), who ranched there prior to the city's westward expansion. An office tower, commercial space, and the Wiltern Theater were built on the corner of Wilshire Boulevard and Western Avenue.

1. Detail of oxidized copper roof of the small tower on the corner of the east elevation.

2. Interior of the theater, which was owned by the Warner Brothers Company. G. Albert Lansburgh collaborated with Stiles O. Clements to create a sumptuous palace of gold leaf and enameled plaster. When the theater failed and was abandoned prior to restoration in 1985 by Brenda Levin Associates, the plaster sunburst on the ceiling had collapsed.

3. General view.

2

3

Wilshire
Denny's
WILTERN

4. Anthony B. Heinsbergen executed the interior decoration, which relies on various permutations of foliage and sunburst motifs.

5. Cove illumination using colors supplements the mezzanine's chandelier.

6. Detail of plaster sconces.

7. Foyer's terrazzo sunburst floor, carved walnut doors, and white metal architraves.

5

6

7

HERSCHEL
1738 – 1822
NEWTON
GRIFFITH OBSERVATORY

GRIFFITH OBSERVATORY

2800 East Observatory Road, Los Angeles, California, 1934–35, John C. Austin and Frederick M. Ashley, architects.

The Griffith Observatory consists of a central pavilion and two flanking wings, each of which originally contained twelve-inch refracting telescopes with coelostats. The central dome contains the planetarium and was illustrated in *The Architect & Engineer*, January 1935, and *Architectural Concrete*, 1936. Griffith is one of three observatories built in the modernistic style (Adler Planetarium in Chicago and Hayden Planetarium in New York City); however, it is the only building to have rigorously maintained architectural integrity. Built of reinforced concrete to resist lateral forces, waste form molds were used, leaving a slight surface texture from the plywood molds. This method reduced the need for hand-finishing other than sanding and washing. Joints were essential to pouring concrete on this scale and were incorporated into the design. The ornamental bronze transom grille continues above the entrance and was produced by A. J. Bayer Co.

1. General view.

2. Observation deck.

3. Detail of foyer roof parapet of bronze.

4. Arcade running along the south elevation has telescopes for viewing the Los Angeles Basin.

1

2

3

4

TICKETS GO ON SALE AT
2:30 P.M.
PLEASE FORM LINE TO THE LEFT
PLANETARIUM
NO SMOKING PLEASE
THE SMOG IS BAD ENOUGH!

5

6

7

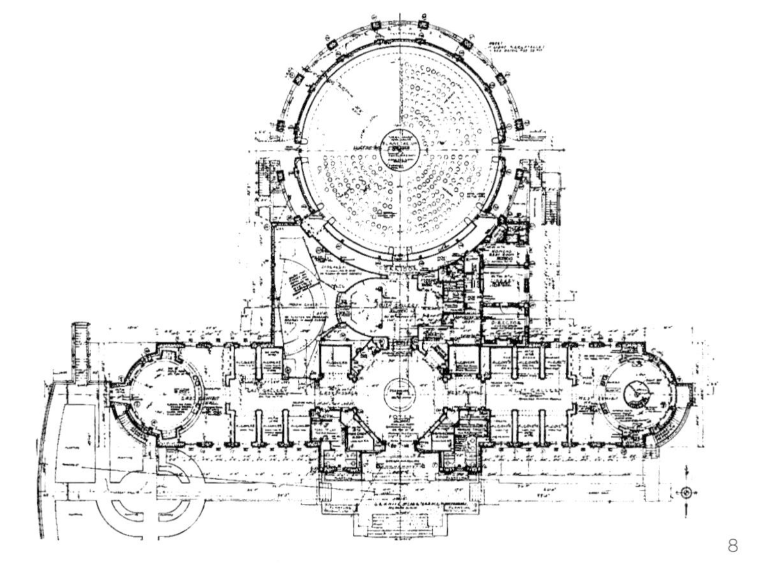

8

5. Foyer walls are travertine. Hugo Ballin painted the foyer murals; the right panel is a group of astronomers: Arzachel, Johannes Sacro Bosco (Hollywood), Copernicus, with Galileo in front.

6. Heinsbergen Decorating Company was responsible for the interior.

7. Navigational and astronomical implements are used as motifs for the bronze door grille.

8. Plan, courtesy of Griffith Observatory.

HONG BUILDINGS

427 and 425 Cinling Way, 951 North Broadway (New Chinatown), Los Angeles, California, 1938, Erle Webster & Adrian Wilson, architects; interior furnishings and furniture by Honor Easton Webster.

2

The Hong Buildings were commissioned by You Chung Hong, who studied law at the University of Southern California and was the first Chinese American in California to pass the bar exam and practice law. Y. C. Hong's office was illustrated in *The Architectural Record,* April 1939. The entrance to Hong's office, 427 Cinling Way, has new gates designed by Hong's son, the architect Roger Hong, AIA, and grandson, Matthew Hong. The Hong buildings fuse modernism with traditional Chinese architecture, probably as a result of Webster & Wilson's study of art and architecture in the collection of Y. C. Hong and his wife, Mabel C. Hong's, personal library. New Chinatown was built in the late 1930s when Old Chinatown was destroyed in order to build Union Station for rail train patrons on its location. New Chinatown was illustrated in *California Arts & Architecture,* October 1939. Webster & Wilson designed numerous buildings, along with an area master plan surrounding its Central Plaza for Los Angeles's New Chinatown.

1. The former Joy Yuen Low Restaurant (currently known as Forbidden City), 425 Cinling Way, the second structure developed by the Hongs, is protected by dragons on the upwardly curving roof over the entrance, juxtaposed with the flamboyant roof of Hong Gallery at 951 North Broadway. The roof tiles were manufactured by Cladding & McBean and given authenticity by Athol McBean's travels in China.

2. General view.

3. The former Joy Yuen Low Restaurant, now Forbidden City, currently under renovation, became a well-known punk-rock and alternative-music venue during the 1980s as well as a location used in various films.

4

5

6

7

4. Roof terrace of Hong's law office. According to traditional Chinese geomancy, which dictates that important buildings face south, You Chung Hong's office building is correctly situated. Hong's office was illustrated in the Chinese Number of *California Arts & Architecture*, October 1939.

5. Tyrus Wong, a well-known Chinese-American artist, was commissioned by Hong to paint the majestic celestial dragon in situ above the west entrance doors and Chinese garden of the Hong Gallery.

6. The East Gate was commissioned by You Chung Hong to honor the memory of his mother, Lee Shee Hong, and is often referred to as the Pailoo of Maternal Virtue or Gate of Filial Piety, honoring her devotion to her family, whom she supported despite privation and the loss of her husband.

7. Detail of entrance marquee on the Joy Yuen Low building.

ICE

AVALON CASINO

I Casino Way, Catalina Island, California, 1928–29, Sumner Spaulding & Walter Webber, architects.

Avalon Casino includes a film theater on the ground floor and a ballroom four stories above street level. The building's owner, William Wrigley, Jr., resolved the complicated problem of access to the ballroom by suggesting the use of ramps similar to those in the Chicago baseball stadium he had recently built. Sumner Spaulding conceived of the Casino as a modernistic design utilizing new materials and equipment. None of the concrete was precast; instead it was poured on location. Other materials, such as the tiles, were manufactured on the island as part of Wrigley's effort to stabilize year-round residency by providing steady employment. The Avalon Casino was illustrated in *California Arts & Architecture*, November 1929.

I. General view.

2. *The Flight of Fancy Westward* asbestos fire curtain symbolizes the progression of William Wrigley, Jr.'s empire, culminating in the acquisition of Catalina Island (intended to preserve its natural heritage). The background, etched in 22-carat gold, is a topographic map, including latitude and longitude. One of the first theaters designed specifically to screen films with sound, the form is almost a true hemisphere. Acoustical engineers F. R Watson and Vern O. Knudsen produced such a successful theater that engineers working on the Radio City Music Hall studied its design. John Gabriel Beckman, with a team of assistants, painted murals on a jute textile stretched from the base of the dome in triangular segments to cover the walls.

3. Concealing the ballroom's ventilation, the thirty-eight-foot-diameter gold-leaf grille supports the light fixtures. N. A. Walburg executed Beckman's design for the decor.

4. A cantilevered fourteen-foot-wide loggia with corbeled arches surrounds the ballroom. It was inspired by the Alhambra in Spain, a building admired by Wrigley, and allows crowds using the ballroom to circulate without interfering with the dance floor.

2

3

4

155 SANSOME

THE STOCK EXCHANGE CLUB

155 Sansome Street, San Francisco, California, 1930, Miller & Pflueger, architects.

Built at the same time Pflueger remodeled the San Francisco Stock Exchange Building, the new building had direct access to the Exchange Building and was ornamented by Ralph Stackpole's monumental sculptures at the entrance. The Stock Exchange Club was illustrated in *The Architect and Engineer*, December 1931.

1. Entrance.

2. The cast-plaster ceiling is gold leaf; the steps lead to a door connected to the Stock Exchange Building.

2

3

4

5

3. Situated on the tenth floor, the dining room has changed little since it was constructed; the ceiling is silver leaf tinged with gold. Michael Goodman was responsible for the interior design. A polished brass and chromium stair balustrade was designed by Goodman. The walls are faced with California travertine.

4. Detail of exterior medallion by Ralph Stackpole.

5. Original furnishings were supplied by W. & J. Sloane.

6. Diego Rivera's mural, *Allegory of California*, fills the stairwell.

PARAMOUNT THEATRE

2025 Broadway, Oakland, California, 1930–31, Miller & Pflueger, architects.

2

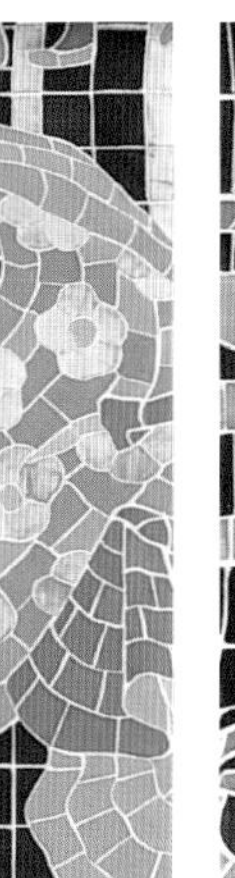

3

4

The Paramount has a mosaic façade rising one hundred feet, intersected by the sign. Mosaic cartoons were produced by Gerald Fitzgerald, an architect with Miller & Pflueger. The *Fountain of Light*, in the grand lobby, designed by Fitzgerald, is sandblasted and etched glass and was conceived to represent water, or the Lotus deity. Behind the *Fountain of Light* is a grille composed of stainless steel fins bent into patterns and illuminated from behind to diffuse light, creating a *Canopy of Light*. The *Canopy of Light* extends the length of the ceiling to the mezzanine and indirectly illuminates the lobby. Production of the metalwork was assisted by Harrison Gill, a consulting architect. *The Architectural Forum*, April 1930, illustrated the theater. Bas-relief painted plaster of the theater auditorium walls was designed by Fitzgerald and executed by Robert B. Howard. The auditorium ceiling is fabricated of metal fins illuminated from behind; lights of various colors are projected against a flat plaster ceiling six feet above the fins and the light is reflected down through and against the sides of the fins. To preserve sight lines, the balcony is suspended from the walls using a large single steel girder. The walls and ceilings of the theater are suspended and curve toward the proscenium to enhance the acoustics. The various surfaces of the metal ceiling and plasterwork produce better acoustics than would a smooth surface.

1. A grand staircase with chrome railings leads up to the mezzanine on each side of the lobby, illuminated with the *Columns of Light*, which are treated optically as false windows. Ornamental metal was produced by Michael & Pfeiffer Iron Works of San Francisco.

2. Detail of mosaics on the façade; cartoons were made by Gerald Fitzgerald; Cladding & McBean produced the tile used.

3. Detail of façade.

4. General view

5. Plan of the main floor.

6. A black marble dado alternates with chrome bands in the lobby. A group of gilded plaster dancers appears in front of each *Column of Light*, probably designed by Theodore Bernardi, who directed the artistic program for the theater.

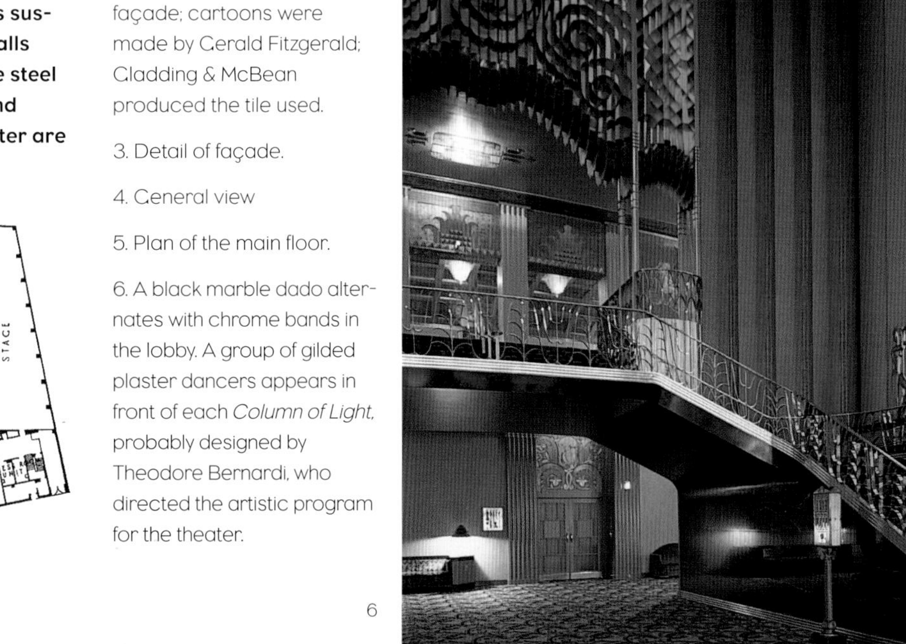

5

6

ALAMEDA COUNTY COURTHOUSE

1221 Oak Street, Oakland, California, 1936, W. G. Corlett, Jas. W. Plachek, Henry A. Minton, William E. Schirmer, and Carl Werner, architects.

2

3

4

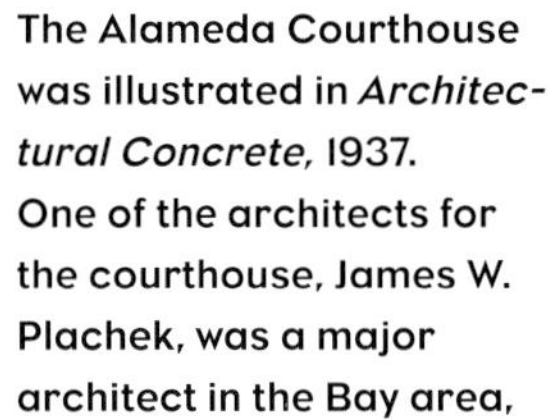

The Alameda Courthouse was illustrated in *Architectural Concrete,* 1937. One of the architects for the courthouse, James W. Plachek, was a major architect in the Bay area, specializing in earthquake resistant construction. He worked in the City Architects' office in San Francisco and the office of W. H. Weeks prior to opening his own practice in Berkeley in 1912 and designed a number of prominent buildings there including schools, a fire-house, and the Berkeley Public Library.

1. General view.

2. Pinnacle.

3. East elevation entrance.

4. American eagle above the south elevation entrance.

1

TEMPLE BETH ISRAEL

1979 Flanders NW, Portland, Oregon, 1924–27, Morris H. Whitehouse & Herman Brookman, John V. Benne & Harry Herzog, architects.

1

2

3

Temple Beth Israel was illustrated in "The Architecture of the Synagogue," *Architecture*, September 1928. A bronze menorah delineates the circular window over the entrance on the west. The basilica dome is reinforced concrete; surrounding walls are illuminated by stained glass windows created by regional artist Albert Gerlach. Black walnut wood details were produced by Nicolai Neppoch Company.

1. Sleek chandeliers with Star of David motifs were designed and fabricated by Fred Baker of Portland.

2. Detail of bronze door handles on entrance; the manner of the shallow incised ornament is similar to a technique used by Tlingit and Eskimo carvings on bone.

3. Chair produced for the foyer.

4. Technically difficult, unusual curved wood seating was produced by American Seating Company, possibly carved by Alois Lang. An advertisement is in *American Architect*, November 1929, for American Seating Company illustrated Temple Beth Israel.

5. Rose window above entrance, terra-cotta ornament was produced by Cladding McBean's Northwestern plant.

4

5

אנכי יהוה
לא יהיה
לא תרצח
לא תנאף

EXIT

5TH AVENUE THEATRE

1308 Fifth Avenue, Seattle, Washington, 1926, Robert C. Reamer, architect; Gustav F. Liljestrom, designer.

2

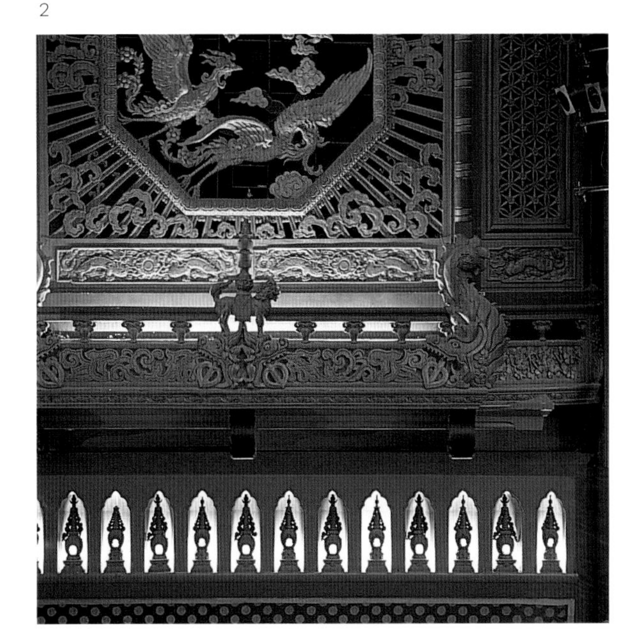

3

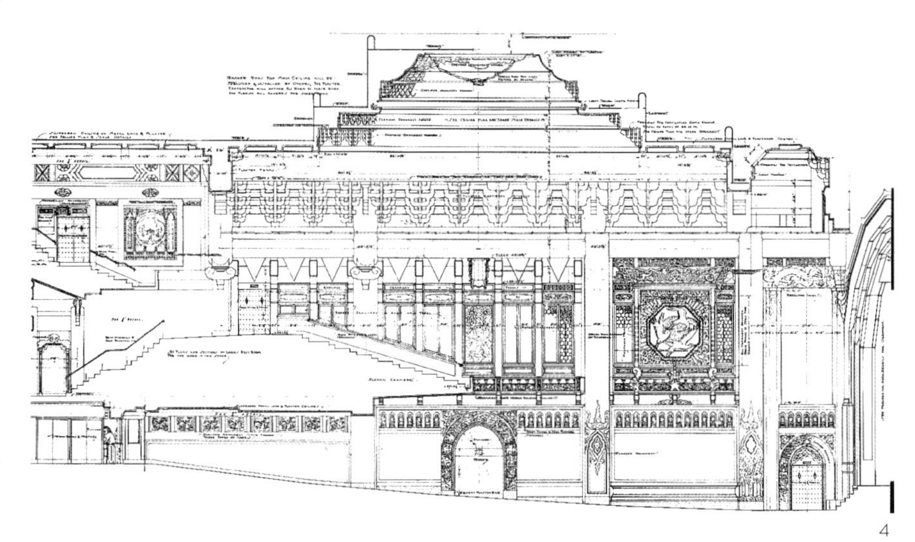

4

The 5th Avenue Theatre is an early project of one of Seattle's preeminent modernistic architects. The theater is located within the Renaissance revival-style Skinner Building, a project published in the February 28, 1927, issue of *Buildings and Building Management*. The project was described in the opening night program: "The Skinner Building—in shops where are marketed together foreign wares and domestic merchandise; in offices, where are administered businesses with extensions over the Seven Seas; in the theater, where are combined the arts of Old World and the New to work a magic of delight—here in this stately edifice, the twain do meet. At the Gateway to the Orient the Skinner Building stands dedicated to the commerce and trade of two great Continents."

1. Inspired by Chinese architecture, specifically, the Summer Palace, the Temple of Heavenly Peace, and the Throne Room of the Imperial Palace in the Forbidden City, the design of the theater was the result of research by Gustav Liljestrom, who lived in China before moving to San Francisco. The tapestries and furniture for the space were commissioned by Liljestrom and imported from China.

2. The Chinese theme is reflected in the merest details.

3. From the mouth of a Great Dragon emanates the chain from which a chandelier is suspended in the auditorium.

4. Section drawing courtesy of the 5th Avenue Theatre.

ST. JOSEPH'S ROMAN CATHOLIC CHURCH

732 Eighteenth Avenue East, Seattle, Washington, 1931, A. H. Albertson, architect, with Joseph W. Wilson & Paul Richardson, associate architects.

1

2

St. Joseph's was illustrated in *Architecture*, February 1931. The church was remarkable at the time for utilizing a novel but economical approach—cast concrete, left unfinished after the concrete forms were removed on the interior and exterior, allowing the construction of a one-thousand-seat capacity building on a budget of $300,000. A mosaic reredos in the church is an austere expression of ornament, appropriate to the Jesuit order for which this church was built.

1. Minimal ornament on the dome is cast stone.

2. Wrought-iron grilles enclose the baptistry, repeating the grape and vine motif used in the painted ornament. The baptistry tabernacle is gold and bronze and was also illustrated in *Architecture*, February 1931.

3. Detail of painted ornament.

4. Plan published in *The Architect & Engineer*, February 1931.

5. Aisles along the nave are ornamented simply, with painted decoration; the wood-paneled confessional is equally unembellished. Using the technique of painted and fired metallic glass, the Stations of the Cross are illuminated by lamps with copper shades.

3

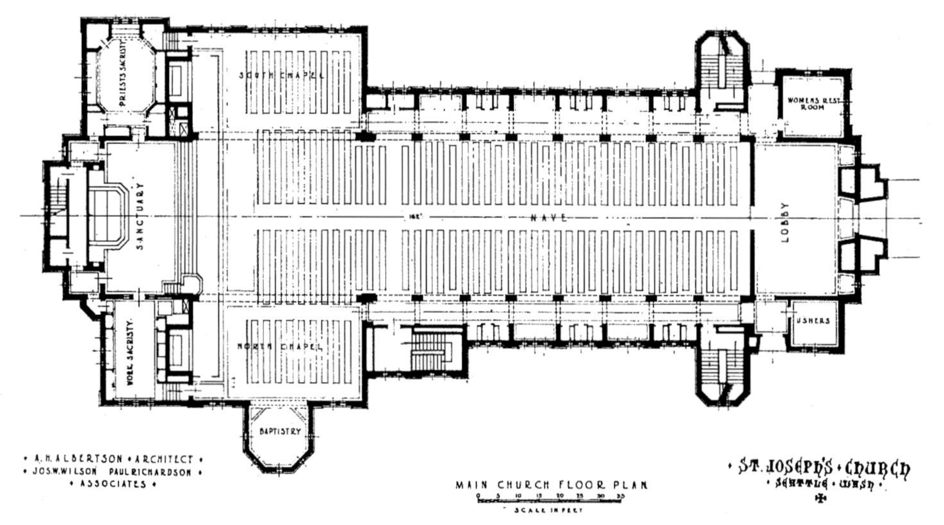

4

FACE TO FACE
LEE KAPPER, S.J.
CONFESSIONS
BEHIND THE
SCREEN
gather

NOTES

INTRODUCTION

1. R. M. Craig, *Atlanta Architecture: Art Deco to Modern Classic, 1929–1959* (Gretna, LA: Pelican Publishing Company, Inc., 1995), 54, illustrates the Evans-Cucich House, designed by A.F.N. Everett, 1934, and described the grand staircase being illuminated by an art deco chandelier "from a New York hotel." Real estate managers and architects have confirmed the existence of this practice during interviews with the author.

2. C. F. McAfee, AIA, *U. S. Post Office and Courthouse, Wichita, Kansas: Feasibility Study for Renovation*, General Services Administration, 1979, is a minute survey of the condition of this building and how it could be modernized at that time, a plan which was not as sensitive to preservation issues as the work ultimately executed.

3. F. L. Wright, "In the Cause of Architecture," *The Architectural Record* (March 1908): 155–65; "In the Cause of Architecture, II. What 'Styles' Mean to the Architect," *The Architectural Record* (February 1928): 145–51. Irving Gill and Robert D. Kohn wrote less frequently than Wright; however, their work was influential and conveyed the concept of simplicity and functionalism as the democratic ideal.

4. B. Sanders, ed., *The Craftsman: An Anthology* (Santa Barbara, CA: Peregrine Smith, 1978). The designer Custav Stickley was editor of this magazine, which frequently contained articles and illustrations pertaining to Native American arts, for instance volumes 16–20, 1909–1911, "Indian Blankets, Baskets and Bowls: The Product of the Original Craftworkers of the Continent," 227–29. "Spontaneous necessity" and an "absolutely natural expression of the individuality of the maker" are terms found in other articles endorsing these indigenous art forms as embodying American qualities. Wildlife sanctuaries, the relation of nonobjective ornament to labor (i.e., *The Theory of the Leisure Class*) and honest design, Tolstoy, Gorky, and "American art purged of artificialities" were frequent topics for discussion among practitioners in the Arts and Crafts Movement.

5. C. Breeze, *Pueblo Deco* (New York: Rizzoli International Publications, Inc., 1990), 99.

6. W. E. Washburn, ed., *Handbook of the American Indian*, vol. 4, *History of Indian-White Relations* (Washington, D.C.: Smithsonian Institution, 1988).

7. R. W. Sexton, *The Logic of Modern Architecture* (New York: Architectural Book Publishing Co., 1929), 48. Underwood's Hotel Apache in Yuma, AZ, was illustrated in a chapter devoted to "The Fundamentals of Architectural Design Applied to Solving Our Modern Problems" as a successful example of a building which reflects purpose.

8. D. Knudsen, "Indian Basketry Art in the Ahwahnee Hotel—Yosemite Valley," *The Architect and Engineer* (November 1928): 51–56.

9. S. E. Gideon, "Shadowgraphs," *Pencil Point* (January 1930) 53–54, describes the process of making photograms using native plants and was inspired by a lecture given by Borglum to the University of Texas Department of Architecture. The article also mentioned that the architects of the new buildings on the campus had already begun to incorporate cattle brands in their decorative work.

10. N. de Brennecke, "Metal Work Designed from Motifs of the American Indian," *American Architect* (December 1930) 24–25, 102.

11. M. Whiffen and C. Breeze, correspondence February–March, 1982, Marcus Whiffen Collection, Arizona State University, Architecture and Environmental Design Library. Discussing the term Pueblo deco, Whiffen argued that it did not encompass Hispanic characteristics, while I argued that the Pueblo style incorporated Spanish Colonial and Mission elements as well as indigenous.

12. "Inspired by Cows and Milk Bottles: The New York Offices of The Walker-Gordon Company," *American Architect* (April 1931): 56–57; Gordon was also published as the architect of a "Smaller Airport," *Pencil Prints*, November 1937, 739–41.

13. B. Byrne, letter to Mark L. Peisch, June 8, 1955, Drawings and Archives at the Avery Architectural and Fine Arts Library. Referring to the influence of the Viennese secession on Maher and others, Byrne wrote: "Re: Ornaments based on local vegetation. This was a sufficiently current practice . . . the design of all of Wright's ornamental glass, which he used to fill the windows of his houses, was a non-literal transcription of indigenous plant forms. . . ."

14. *Pavilions étrangers sur le Course-la-Reine*, Exposition des Arts Décoratifs et Industriels Modernes of 1925, unpaginated plates.

15. N. J. Troy, *Modernism and the Decorative Arts in France: Art Nouveau to Le Corbusier* (New Haven: Yale University Press, 1991), 101.

16. T. Veblen, *The Theory of the Leisure Class* (New York: Macmillan, 1899; reprint, New York: Viking Press, 1931, 160.

17. M. Whiffen, *American Architecture Since 1780: A Guide to the Styles* (Cambridge: The MIT Press, 1992; revised edition): 149.

18. H. Meiere, "The Question of Decoration," *Architectural Forum* (July 1932): 2.

19. "Portfolio," *The Metal Arts* (November 1928).

20. *Atlantic Terra Cotta* (January 1928): 19.

21. E. Clute, "Techniques in Modern Mosaics," *The Architectural Forum* (January 1932) 72–75, explains that Cosmati mosaics are larger and the forms or mosaic units (referred to as tesserae) can include shapes such as triangular, oblong, and irregular. Two Park Avenue is also illustrated.

22. Clute, "Modern Mosaics," 142.

23. E. Clute, "Design Possibilities in Metal," *The Architectural Forum* (February 1932): 147–50, discussed the use of metal and illustrated (among others) the Union Trust Building in Detroit, Sloan & Robertson's 29 Broadway, and Kenneth Franzheim's 22 East Fortieth Street building in New York City.

24. E. Clute, "Glass Mosaic," *Architecture* (September 1931): 141–46; E. Clute, "Designed for Easy Fabricating: Irving Trust Company Building," *American Architect* (November 1931): 42–47

25. Clute, 143.

26. Clute, 146. Ravenna Mosaics used tesserae produced in Berlin, and was associated with Puhl Wagner Mosaic Company there. Ralph Walker and Perry Coke Smith of Voorhees, Gmelin & Walker visited the studio in Berlin to order the tesserae.

27. Clute, 143.

28. "One Wall Street," *The Kaleidoscope* (April 1931): 7–13; E. Clute, "Modern Decorative Light Sources," *Architecture*, August 1931: 73.

29. R. Horn (restoration artist), interview by author, Chicago, Illinois, August 6, 2001.

30. E. H. Reed, "Edgar Miller, Designer-Craftsman," *Architecture* (August 1932): 68.

31. Ibid.

32. L. Bruner, "Edgar Miller: A Versatile Artist & Craftsman," *American Artist* (May 1963) 38–43, 65–67.

33. C. C. Rambusch, "Rambusch: Ninety Years of Art Metal," *The Journal for Decorative Arts and Propaganda*, 33.

34. "Alois Lang, Wood Carver," *Architecture* (February 1934): 103.

35. "Alois Lang," 106.

36. "Alois Lang," 103.

THE NORTHEAST

1. Federal Writers' Project, *New York Panorama* (New York: Pantheon, 1984), 88; original copyright 1938, the Guilds' Committee for Federal Writers' Publications, Inc.

2. *New York Panorama*, 82–131.

3. F. L. Allen, *Only Yesterday: An Informal History of the 1920's* (1964; reprint, New York: Harper & Row, 1982), 239.

4. T. Crane, *Architectural Construction: The Choice of Structural Design*, 2d ed. (New York: John Wiley & Sons, Inc., 1947): 24. The term *curtain wall* affirms its relative insubstantiality and its analogy to textiles.

5. R.A.M. Stern, G. Gilmartin, T. Mellins, *New York 1930: Architecture and Urbanism Between the Two World Wars*, 34–37 (New York: Rizzoli International Publications, Inc., 1997).

6. R. Bletter, "Metropolis réduite," *Archithese* 18 (1976): 22–27.

7. Allen, *Only Yesterday*, 149. The author considered the association of religion and business to be a major phenomenon of the 1920s.

8. Allen, *Only Yesterday*.

9. Allen, *Only Yesterday*.

10. R. S. Lynd and H. M. Lynd, *Middletown* (New York: Harcourt, Brace & Company, 1929), 315.

11. R. A. Orsi, *The Madonna of 115th Street: Faith and Community in Italian Harlem, 1880–1950* (New Haven: Yale University Press, 1985) p. xix. Accompanying Italian immigrants were the differing devotions particular to each region or village. For example, La Madonna del Carmine was the protector of Polla, a village in the province of Salerno. Mutual aid societies were often formed and named for these patron saints, and ultimately in the United States organized under parish clerical authority, eventually becoming an official congregation, and consequently to the construction of a church dedicated to the organization's saint (p. 53).

12. *Ecclesiastical Arts* 2, no. 2 (1933), advertisement, unpaginated.

13. "Church of the Most Precious Blood, Astoria, New York City," *American Architect* 142, no. 2614 (December 1932): 59–68.

14. C. F. Bragdon, *Architecture and Democracy* (New York: Alfred A. Knopf, 1918), 82. Bragdon also wrote *The Frozen Fountain*, 1932, which describes the impact of modernistic architecture and ornament.

15. Bragdon, *Architecture and Democracy*, 103.

16. Bragdon, *Architecture and Democracy*.

17. R. Walker, "A New Architecture," *Architectural Forum* (January 1928): 3–4.

18. T. Veblen, *The Theory of the Leisure Class* (New York: Macmillan, 1899; reprint, New York: Viking Press, 1931), 127–28.

19. C. Breeze, *New York Deco* (New York: Rizzoli, 1992), 33.

20. Breeze, *New York Deco*, 20.

THE SOUTH

1. "Caddo Parish Courthouse, Shreveport, Louisiana," *American Architect* (August 1929): 145–46.

2. M. McDonough, "Selling Sarasota: Architecture and Propaganda in a 1920's Boom Town," *The Journal of Decorative Arts and Propaganda* (Florida issue, 1998): 11.

3. "New Prison for the State of Georgia: Tatnall County on the Ohoopee River, Tucker & Howell, Architects, Atlanta, Georgia" (March 1937): 13–17.

4. *Stone* (May 1934): 199, U.S. Post Office Building, High Point, NC, Everhart, Voorhees, Workman & Eckles, architects.

5. Johnson & Brannan, architects, advertisement for Tompkins-Kiel Marble Co., New York, Virginia Greenstone quarried in soapstone district near Lynchburg, floors 1–4 and spandrels of this material.

6. F. L. Allen, *Only Yesterday* (1931); reprint, New York: Harper & Row, 1964), 149.

7. L. Cerwinski, "A Touch of the Orient, Reviving a Sixty-year-old Miami Fantasy," *Southern Accents*: 114–123.

8. F. E. Thomson, III, Asheville Museum of Art, text attached to drawings in collection, unpaginated, undated.

9. S. Middleton (niece of Douglas Ellington and current resident of his house on Chunn's Cove), interview by author, April 22, 2001.

10. Middleton interview.

11. Middleton interview.

12. Middleton interview.

13. J. M. Schorrenberg, *Remembered Past, Discovered Future: The Alabama Architecture of Warren, Knight & Davis, 1906–1961* (Birmingham, AL: Birmingham Museum of Art, 1999), 1–22.

14. Schorrenberg, *Remembered Past*, 68.

15. E. J. Jolly, *Pelican Guide to the Louisiana Capitol* (Gretna, LA: Pelican Publishing Co., 1980), 9.

16. Jolly, *Pelican Guide*, 16–17.

17. Jolly, *Pelican Guide*, 117.

18. D. Hayden, *The Grand Domestic Revolution* (Cambridge, MA: MIT Press, 1981), 72–77.

19. R. M. Craig, *Atlanta Architecture: Art Deco to Modern Classic, 1929–1959* (Gretna, LA: Pelican Publishing Company, Inc., 1995), 37–40.

THE MIDWEST AND PRAIRIES

1. S. Lewis, *Babbitt* (New York: NAL Penguin, 1970 edition) 14.

2. "Millions Involved in Deal on Circle," *Indianapolis Sunday Star* (December 30, 1928): 1.

3. "Office Rental Booklets," *National Real Estate Journal* (April 14, 1930): 57.

4. E. H. Krause, "Trademarks and Symbols," *Design* (March 1937): 8–10. Erik Hans Kraus, a graphic designer, created logos for various textile products and companies; writing about the process of designing a logo, he remarked, "Symbolic designs are really the first manifestations of man's culture, as they were a medium of expression before any written language was evolved. Even then, they proved indispensable to the expression of abstract matter [corporate integrity, innovation, etc.]."

5. C. Pitts, *National Register of Historic Places Registration Form*, sec. 8, February 9, 1989.

6. A. Lee, "The Chicago Daily News Building," *Architectural Forum* (August 1931): 21.

7. Lee, "Chicago Daily News," 22

8. Lee, "Chicago Daily News."

9. F. L. Allen, *Only Yesterday* (1931; reprint, New York: Harper & Row, 1964), p. 136.

10. "Woodbury County Courthouse, Sioux City, Iowa, William L. Steele, Architect, Purcell & Elmslie, Associate Architect," *The Western Architect*, (February 1921): 14. The terra-cotta ornament of the Woodbury County Courthouse is quite Sullivanesque, and is the contribution of Purcell & Elmslie. William Steele also designed the First Congregational Church in Sioux City, located near the courthouse, which was extremely progressive in its restrained use of ornament and emphasis on volumes. The church was published in *The Western Architect* (January 1919): plates 1–5.

11. J. Paterek, *Encyclopedia of American Indian Costume* (New York: W. W. Norton, 1994), 87.

12. Stewart-Taylor Company, *Naniboujou Lodge*, reproduction of original brochure printed in 1928, Duluth, Minnesota, unpaginated.

13. T. Raney, interview by author, June 17, 2001.

14. "Work at Club of Naniboujou Progressing," *Cook County News-Herald*, (August 9, 1928): 1.

15. "Naniboujou Club Opened Sunday," *Cook County News-Herald*, (July 11, 1929): 1.

16. A. M. Hutting, *Shrine of the Little Flower* (1936; reprint, Royal Oak, Michigan: Radio League of the Little Flower, 1998), 5.

17. *The New Municipal Auditorium, Kansas City, Missouri*, introduction of brochure, unpaginated.

18. F. L. Wright, "In the Cause of Architecture," *The Architectural Record* (March 1908): 157.

19. F. C. Luebke, "The Capitals and Capitols of Nebraska," *The Nebraska State Capitol* (Lincoln, NE: University of Nebraska Press, 1990), 13.

20. M. D. Masters, *Hartley Burr Alexander—Writer in Stone* (Lincoln, NE: Jacob North Printing Co., 1992), 51.

21. Masters, *Hartley Burr Alexander*, 51–52.

22. L. M. Dunn, unpublished manuscript, 9. Dunn, Meiere's daughter, includes portions of Meiere's unpublished autobiography, *My Life and Times: Not Hard*, in this manuscript.

23. C.W.J. Beal, *Joslyn Art Museum: A Building History* (Omaha, NE: Joslyn Art Museum, 1997), 36. Alexander criticized Brcin's work as "too Slavic," and, in the process of reorienting the sculptural program, removed rearing horses Brcin conceived to flank the entrance.

24. H. Hite and M. Weiseger, Oklahoma County Courthouse, Oklahoma City, Oklahoma, National Register of Historic Places Nomination Form, 1991.

25. "The Boston Avenue Methodist-Episcopal Church, South, Tulsa, Oklahoma: Rush, Endacott & Rush, Architects; Bruce Goff, Designer; Adah M. Robinson, Associate," *Architectural Record* (December 1929): 519–524.

26. D. G. De Long, *Bruce Goff: Toward an Absolute Architecture* (Cambridge: MIT Press, 1988), 13. Additionally, the parapet of the 1925 Tulsa Building, designed by Goff, bears a resemblance to the parapet of the auditorium of the Boston Avenue Methodist-Episcopal Church. Attribution of the design of the church became so contentious that Rush, Endacott & Rush ultimately resorted to legal counsel and obtained an affidavit attesting to the their firm's role as sole architects (p. 30).

27. A. Cole, letter to Mr. Pigford, June 8, 1937, courtesy of Boston Avenue United Methodist-Episcopal Church archives.

28. Original drawings for these details are located in Boston Avenue United Methodist Episcopal Church archives.

29. "The Boston Avenue Methodist Episcopal Church, South, Tulsa, Oklahoma: Rush, Endacott, Architects; Bruce Goff, Designer; Adah M. Robinson, Associate," *Architectural Record* (November 1929): 519–524.

THE SOUTHWEST

1. R. N. Ellis, *New Mexico Past and Present: A Historical Reader* (Albuquerque: University of New Mexico Press, 1971): 5.

2. D. Gebhard, "Architecture and the Fred Harvey House," *New Mexico Architecture* (July–August 1962): 12.

3. S. D'Emilio and S. Campbell, *Visions & Visionaries: The Art & Artists of the Santa Fe Railway* (Salt Lake City: Peregrine Smith, 1991) 24.

4. R. Henderson, "The Spanish-Indian Tradition in Interior Decoration," *Architectural Record* (January–June 1927): 189. Another article by the same author, "The American Indian's Contribution to Design: Our Indigenous Art Should Furnish Vitality and Diversity to the Modern Movement," *House Beautiful* (April 1930): 437, 486–89, also promoted the art and architecture of the Southwest.

5. D'Emilio and Campbell, *Visions & Visionaries*, 2. Capitalizing on the ubiquity of this advertising campaign, the American Alcohol Corporation placed a series of advertisements which were a parody of the Santa Fe Railroad's. "See American First" appeared in numerous issues of *The Modern Hospital* during the late 1920s through the 1930s, and were illustrated by a different silhouette in each issue—an Indian with a feather in a headband, Daniel Boone, or a forty-niner—accompanied by a brief paragraph of American history. *Modern Hospital* (November 1929): 131.

6. C. H. Dorr, "Sculpture and Mural Painting of the Missouri State Capitol," *Architectural Record* (February 1927): 121–26, illustrates the impact of AT&SF Railroad's advertising campaign. E. Irving Couse, Ernest L. Blumenschein, Oscar Berninghaus, and Bert Phillips were engaged to paint the murals for the Missouri State Capitol building.

7. R. Henderson, "A Primitive Basis for Modern Architecture," *Architectural Record* (August 1923): 196. E. Irving Couse's "Moonlight, Pueblo de Taos," on p. 187, is one of the illustrations for the article that romantically portrays the Native American. "Living always in close communion with earth and sky, the Indian felt a mystic charm in the simplest natural objects. He observed with uncanny accuracy and reflected in poetic symbols the truth and beauty as he saw it" (p. 202).

8. R. Henderson, "A Primitive Basis," 188.

9. J. A. Droege, *Passenger Terminals and Trains* (New York: McGraw Hill, 1916), 12.

10. "New Indian-Detours," advertisement for the Santa Fe Railroad, *International Studio* (1930): 127, features a photograph of an inhabitant wrapped in a blanket at Taos Pueblo. The text reads, "What is an Indian-Detour? It Is the most Distinctive Motor Service in the World. It is the deluxe way—by Cadillac Harveycar—of visiting the hidden primitive Spanish Missions, old Mexican villages, colorful Indian pueblos, prehistoric cliffdwellings and buried cities—all set in the matchless scenery and climate of the Southern Rockies."

11. A. Berke, *Mary Colter: Architect of the Southwest*, (New York: Princeton Architectural Press, 2002), 56. Berke's biography is an expansion and addition of material originally published by V. L. Gratton, *Mary Colter: Builder Upon the Red Earth* (Flagstaff, Arizona: Northland Press, 1980).

12. Maisel Building file, John Gaw Meem records, Special Collections, Zimmerman Library, University of New Mexico.

13. Maisel Building file.

14. D. D. Dunn, *American Indian Painting of the Southwest and Plains* (Albuquerque: University of New Mexico Press), 1968.

15. Luhr's Tower was published in *American Architect* (May 1930): 58. Illustrating Henderson's "A Primitive Basis for Modern Architecture" were two buildings, the Franciscan Hotel, designed by Trost & Trost, and architect Alfred C. Bossom's apartment in New York City, which is described in the article. "Alfred C. Bossom, the New York architect, though an Englishman by birth and early training, has become much interested in American Indian cuture and has even evolved his own totem pole. He has finished and furnished his New York apartment in an adaptation of the Spanish-Indian style" (p. 197); "Mr. Bossom has caught something of the poetic largeness of this distinctively American mode. . . ." (p. 198).

16. The Handbook of Texas Online: Fair Park, www.tsha.utexas.edu/handbook/online/articles, November 25, 2000, 7:34 P.M., 1.

17. R. E. Brooks and J. C. Henry, "George L. Dahl and the Texas Centennial Exposition," *Perspective* (December 1981): 9.

18. A. C. McArthur, Jr., "The Hotel Near Phoenix, 1928–29," *Triglyph*, Fall, 1997, "By the end of 1927 Albert Chase McArthur had finished the last sketches and preliminary elevation studies for the Arizona Biltmore, and had decided it should be built using the textile-bloc slab construction method which Frank Lloyd Wright had used for several houses in California. As someone thought that Wright had patents on the method, the Arizona Biltmore attorneys required that a release be obtained for their use. So in January 1928 Albert Chase wrote to Wright, asking permission to use the method and offering a $10,000 release fee. Wright telegraphed his reply." Indicating that he should come out to Arizona to assist McArthur, "Wright was hired as Albert Chase's personal consultant on the block construction at the same wage as his senior draftsman. He had no choice but to accept the job, as he had no money after the bank took over Taliesin in Wisconsin." Wright stayed for four tumultuous months during which period he and McArthur argued constantly. Wright was ultimately dismissed. Subsequently, as Wright began to assume design credit for the Biltmore publicly, he was forced to write a statement retracting this claim (p. 45).

In a May,1963 excerpt from "Parabiography" of Purcell and Elmslie—1912, William Gray Purcell sent to Mark L. Peisch, May, 1953, "Let me give one example or two of Wright's unwillingness to give any credit whatsoever to the contributions of others to his projects. For example, on one of his houses he said to Walter B. Griffin, who was virtually an unacknowledged partner of Wright's at that time, "We'll have a little contest. You do one [design for a house], I'll do one—see which one is best. Griffin solved the project with so unique a solution, that Wright had to acknowledge it in toto—and the house was carried to completion under Griffin's direction. No acknowledgment! Griffin's name was never mentioned by Wright, although Griffin made very extensive and basic contributions to many of Wright's projects." Drawings and Archives at the Avery Architectural and Fine Arts Library, Mark L. Peisch Collection.

19. Brooks and Henry, "George L. Dahl."

20. M. McCullar, "Profile: George L. Dahl, FAIA, Dallas Designer, Innovator, Entrepreneur," *Texas Architect* (November–December 1980): 74.

21. J. I. Fortune, "Texas Centennial: A New Note in Exposition Architecture," *The Architect & Engineer* (February 1936): 17.

22. D. Grafly, "Interview with Pierre Bourdelle," *American Artist* (May 1952): 46.

23. D. Grafly, "Pierre Bourdelle," 47.

24. Brooks and Henry, "George L. Dahl."

25. Biography of Carlo Ciampaglia, Centennial Exposition files, Biographies, Dallas Historical Archives, unpaginated, includes a summary of his career prior to 1936. He was born in Italy in 1891 and immigrated to the United States when he was a child. Ciampaglia produced sketches and the color scheme for Raymond Hood's Masonic Temple in Scranton, Pennsylvania, residential work for various clients, and was a member of the National Academy of Design.

26. J. B. Larrinaga to G. Dahl, interoffice communication regarding the techniques to be used for the murals, August 13, 1935.

27. Larrinaga to Dahl.

28. J. I. Fortune, 15.

29. *Pencil Points* (February 1936): 61.

CALIFORNIA AND THE PACIFIC NORTHWEST

1. W. F. Paris, "The International Exposition of Modern Industrial and Decorative Art in Paris," *The Architectural Record* (October 1925): 370.

2. D. Albrecht, *Designing Dreams: Modern Architecture in the Movies* (New York: Harper & Row, 1986), 40.

3. J. I. Fortune, "Texas Centennial: A New Note in Exposition Architecture," *The Architect & Engineer* (February 1936): 17.

4. Fortune, "Texas Centennial."

5. Juan B. Larrinaga biography, Dallas Historical Society Archives for the Texas Centennial, unpaginated.

6. Fortune, "Texas Centennial."

7. R. Alleman, *The Movie Lover's Guide to Hollywood* (New York: Harper & Row, 1985), 177.

8. D. Gebhard, *Robert Stacy-Judd: Maya Architecture and the Creation of a New Style* (Santa Barbara: Capra Press, 1993), 39.

9. D. Knudsen, "Indian Basketry Art in the Ahwahnee Hotel—Yosemite Valley," *The Architect & Engineer* (November 1928): 51–56.

10. A Santa Fe Railroad advertisement for the Chief, a luxury train with Pullman accommodations traveling from Chicago to Los Angeles, featured an illustration of a stylized Chinese woman, captioned " 'Blossom Time' All the Time in California," *International Studio* (November 1930): 98.

11. L. See, *On Gold Mountain* (New York: Vintage, 1995), 80–88. Suie One Company, owned by Fong See, owned stores in Los Angeles, Pasadena, and Long Beach, which were patronized by Charles and Henry Green, among others.

12. K. H. Hamilton, "The Influence of Chinese Art on Modern Interior Decoration," *The Architect & Engineer* (January 1926): 74.

13. See, *On Gold Mountain*, 214.

14. New Chinatown was illustrated in *California Arts & Architecture*, October 1939. Webster & Wilson designed numerous buildings, including an area master plan surrounding its Central Plaza for Los Angeles's New Chinatown.

15. C. H. Crane, "Observations on Motion Picture Theaters," *The Architectural Record* (June 1925): 381.

16. J. C. Austin, "The Los Angeles City Hall," *Architectural Forum* (September 1928): 25.

17. Austin, "Los Angeles."

18. A. H. Larsen, "Apartment House Financing," *The Architect & Engineer* (December 1930): 39.

19. Larsen, "Apartment House."

20. J. S. Taylor, "New Trends in Home Design," *The Architect & Engineer* (August 1929): 87.

21. "Northern Life Tower," *Shapes of Clay* (November 1929): 4.

22. "Northern Life Tower."

23. *Northern Life Tower* (Seattle: Northern Life Tower, 1929), unpaginated.

24. *Northern Life Tower.*

25. *Northern Life Tower.*

26. Mrs. John Puninton Fay, "Gould, Carl Frelinghuysen, Architect, Art Connoisseur, Educator, Civic Leader," *Encyclopedia of American Biography* (copy of text in the Carl F. Gould Architects reference file, University of Washington Library Archives).

27. A. G. Hauberg, interview by author, December 13, 2001. Gould Hauberg remembered this incident was related by her father, who felt the aluminum requirement could only be attributed to the fact that the Secretary of Treasury at the time was Andrew W. Mellon. Mellon was Secretary of Treasury from 1921 under President Harding until he left President Hoover's cabinet in 1932. Mellon was a major stockholder of the Aluminum Company of America during his tenure as Secretary, so Gould's anecdote may have credibility.

28. Carl F. Gould Drawing Collection, University of Washington Archives.

29. W. Crowley, *National Trust Guide: Seattle* (New York: John Wiley & Sons, 1998), 6.

30. *The Story of the Bon Marché* (Seattle: Western Printing Co; illustrations by Ernest N. Norling and graphic design by Emmet Ewers and Glenn Sheckles, 1929); unpaginated. (From John Graham, Sr., Architects, reference file, University of Washington Archives.)

31. *The Story of the Bon Marché.*

32. *The Story of the Bon Marché.*

33. *The Story of the Bon Marché.*

34. Opening Night Program, Fifth Avenue Theatre, 1.

35. Opening Night Program.

36. Opening Night Program.

BIBLIOGRAPHY

Andrews, Wayne, *Architecture in Chicago and Mid-America* (New York: Harper & Row), 1968.

Arwas, Victor, *Art Deco* (New York: Harry N. Abrams, Inc.), 1992.

Bach, Ira J., and Susan Wolfson, *Chicago on Foot* (Chicago: Chicago Review Press), 1987.

Balfour, Alan, *Rockefeller Center: Architecture as Theater* (New York: McGraw-Hill), 1978.

Banham, Reyner, *Theory & Design in the First Machine Age* (Cambridge: The MIT Press), 2d ed., 1980.

Barron, Stephanie, Sheri Bernstein, and Ilene Susan Fort, *Made in California: Art, Image, and Identity, 1900–2000* (Berkeley: University of California Press and Los Angeles County Museum of Art), 2000.

Battersby, Martin, *The Decorative Thirties* (London: Studio Vista), 1971.

Bayer, Patricia, *Art Deco Interiors: Decoration and Design Classics of the 1920s and 1930s* (London: Thames & Hudson), 1990.

Beal, Graham W. J., *Joslyn Art Museum: A Building History* (Omaha: The Joslyn Art Museum), 1997.

Bennett, T. P., *Architectural Design in Concrete* (London: E. Benn, Ltd.), 1927.

Berkhofer, Robert F., Jr., "White Conception of Indians," *Handbook of North American Indians* (Washington: Smithsonian Institution), 1988.

Blake, Peter, *The Master Builders: Le Corbusier, Mies van der Rohe, Frank Lloyd Wright* (New York: W. W. Norton), 1976.

Blaney, Donald E., and Paul E. Sprague, Immaculata High School, National Register of Historic Places Inventory-Nomination Form, 1977.

Boller Brothers Architectural Records, Joint Collection Western Historical Manuscript Collection, State Historical Society of Missouri Manuscripts, Kansas City.

Bonnifield, Mathew P., *The Dust Bowl* (Albuquerque: University of New Mexico Press), 1979.

Bradley, John D., and Martha Jo Bradley, "Dr. Adah M. Robinson-Designer," Unpublished ms.

Bragdon, Claude, *A Primer of Higher Space* (New York: Alfred A. Knopf), 1913.

——, *Four Dimensional Vistas* (New York: Alfred A. Knopf), 1916.

——, *Architecture and Democracy* (New York: Alfred A. Knopf), 1918.

——, *The Frozen Fountain* (New York: Alfred A. Knopf), 1932.

Breeze, Carla, Introduction by Rosemarie Haag Bletter, *New York Deco* (New York: Rizzoli International), 1993.

——, Introduction by David Gebhard, *L. A. Deco* (New York: Rizzoli International), 1991.

——, *Pueblo Deco* (New York: Rizzoli International), 1990.

Brooks, H. Allen, *The Prairie School: Frank Lloyd Wright and His Midwest Contemporaries* (New York: W. W. Norton), 1972.

Bruegmann, Robert, *Holabird & Roche and Holabird & Root* (New York: Garland Publishing, Inc.), 1992.

Bush, Donald J., *The Streamlined Decade* (New York: George Braziller), 1975.

Canon, Patricia D., Egyptian Theatre, National Register of Historic Places Inventory-Nomination Form, 1978.

Capitman, Barbara, *Deco Delights: Preserving the Beauty and Joy of Miami Beach Architecture* (New York: E.P. Dutton), 1988.

Capitman, Barbara, Michael D. Kinerk, and Dennis W. Wilhelm, *Rediscovering Art Deco U.S.A.* (New York: Viking Studio Books), 1994.

Chappell, Sally A. Kitt, *Architecture and Planning of Graham, Anderson, Probst and White, 1912–1936: Transforming Tradition,* (Chicago: The University of Chicago Press), 1992.

Cheney, Sheldon, *The New World Architecture* (New York: Longmans, Green), 1930.

Christian, Ralph J., Chicago Board of Trade Building, Chicago, Illinois, National Register of Historic Places Inventory-Nomination Form, 1975.

——, Marshall Field & Company Store, Chicago, Illinois, National Register of Historic Places Inventory-Nomination Form, 1977.

Cohen, Judith, *Cowtown Moderne: Art Deco Architecture of Fort Worth, Texas* (College Station: Texas A & M University Press), 1988.

Conn, Richard, *Circles of the World: Traditional Art of the Plains Indians* (Denver: Denver Art Museum), 1982.

Craig, Robert M., *Atlanta Architecture: Art Deco to Modern Classic, 1929–1959* (Gretna, Louisiana: Pelican Publishing Company, Inc.), 1995.

Crane, Theodore, *Architectural Construction* (New York: John Wiley & Sons), 1956.

Crowe, Michael F., *Deco by the Bay: Art Deco Architecture in the San Francisco Bay Area* (New York: Viking Studio Books), 1995.

Dolkart, Andrew S., *Forging a Metropolis* (New York: Whitney Museum of American Art), 1990.

Dorsey, James Owen, "Siouan Sociology," *Bureau of American Ethnology* (Washington: Government Printing Office)15th ed, 1897.

DeLong, David G., *Bruce Goff: Toward Absolute Architecture* (New York: The Architectural History Foundation), 1988.

Duncan, Alastair, *American Art Deco* (London: Thames & Hudson Ltd.), 1986.

Eckert, Kathryn Bishop, *Cranbrook* (New York: Princeton Architectural Press), 2001.

Editors of Look and Louis Bromfield, *Look at America: The Midwest* (Boston: The Houghton Mifflin Company), 1947.

Ehrlich, George, *Kansas City, Missouri: An Architectural History 1826–1976* (Kansas City: Historic Kansas City Foundation), 1979.

Federal Writers Project, *New York Panorama* (New York: Pantheon), 1984.

Ferry, W. Hawkins, *The Buildings of Detroit* (Detroit: Wayne State University Press), 1968.

Fitch, James Marston, *American Building: The Historical Forces That Shaped It* (New York: Schocken) 2d ed. revised, 1973.

Frampton, Kenneth, *Modern Architecture: A Critical History* (New York: Oxford University Press), 1980.

Frankl, Paul T., *Form and Re-Form* (New York: Harper & Brothers), 1930.

Gantz, Richard, *Historic Indiana,* (Indianapolis: Indian Department of Natural Resources).

Garner, John S., ed., *The Midwest in American Architecture* (Urbana and Chicago: University of Illinois Press), 1991.

Gebhard, David, *Tulsa Deco: An Architectural Era, 1925–1942,* Introduction (Tulsa: Junior League of Tulsa, Inc.), 1980.

——, *The National Trust Guide to Art Deco in America* (New York: John Wiley & Sons), 1996.

Gebhard, David, and Robert Winter, *Architecture in Los Angeles: A Compleat Guide* (Salt Lake City: Peregrine Smith), 1985.

Gebhard, David and Harriette von Breton, *L.A. In the Thirties,* (Salt Lake City: Peregrine Smith), 1975.

Gill, Brendan, *Many Faces: A Life of Frank Lloyd Wright* (New York: G.P. Putnam's Sons), 1987.

Gilman, Charlotte Perkins, *Herland* (New York: Pantheon Books), 1979.

Green, Rayna, "The Indian in Popular American Culture," *Handbook of North American Indians* (Washington: Smithsonian Institution), 1988.

Griffin, Marion Mahoney, "The Magic of America," unpublished manuscript, New York Historical Society, September 30, 1949.

——, Letter to W. G. Purcell, August 7, 1947 (Avery Library Archives).

Harris, Jo Beth, *More Than a Building: The First Century of Boston Avenue United Methodist Church* (Tulsa, Oklahoma: Council Oak Publishing Co.), 1993.

Hagedorn-Krass, Martha, Hollywood Theater, Leavenworth, Kansas, National Register of Historic Places Registration Form, 1990.

——, Anthony Theater, Anthony, Kansas, National Register of Historic Places Registration Form, 1990.

——, Augusta Theater, Augusta, Kansas, National Register of Historic Places Registration Form, 1990.

——, Fox Theater, Hutchinson, Kansas. National Register of Historic Places Registration Form, 1989.

——, Fox-Watson Theater Building, Salina, Kansas, National Register of Historic Places Registration Form, 1988.

——, Reno County Courthouse, Hutchinson, Kansas, National Register of Historic Places Registration Form, 1986.

Hassrick, Royal B., *The Sioux: Life and Customs of a Warrior Society* (Norman: University of Oklahoma Press), 1964.

Hayden, Dolores, *Redesigning the American Dream: The Future of Housing, Work, and Family Life* (New York: W. W. Norton & Company), 1984.

Henderson, Linda Dalrymple, *The Fourth Dimension and Non-Euclidean Geometry in Modern Art* (Princeton: Princeton University Press), 1983.

Hillier, Bevis and Escritt, Stephen, *Art Deco Style* (London: Phaidon).

Hitchcock, Henry-Russell, *In the Nature of Materials: The Buildings of Frank Lloyd Wright 1887–1941* (New York: Da Capo Press), 1986.

Hitchcock, H. R., and P. Johnson, *The International Style: Architecture since 1922* (New York: W. W. Norton & Company), 1932.

Hite, Harold A., and Marsha Weisiger, Oklahoma County Courthouse, Oklahoma City, Oklahoma, National Register of Historic Places Registration Form, 1991.

——, *Great Buildings Ahead: A Walking and Motoring Tour of Central Oklahoma Architecture* (Oklahoma City: American Institute of Architects, Oklahoma City Chapter, and Metropolitan Library System), 1989.

Homer, William I., *Alfred Stieglitz and the American Avant Garde* (Boston: New York Graphic Society), 1977.

Hooker, Van Dorn, and Melissa Howard, *Only in New Mexico: An Architectural History of the University of New Mexico* (Albuquerque: University of New Mexico Press), 2000.

Jolly, Ellen Roy, and James Calhoun, *The Louisiana Capitol* (Gretna, Louisiana: Pelican Publishing Company), 1998.

June, Glory, *Art Deco in Indianapolis* (Indianapolis: Indiana Architectural Foundation), 1980.

Kilham, Walter H., *Raymond Hood, Architect; Form Through Function–The American Skyscraper* (New York: Architectural Book Publishing Co.), 1973.

King, Mary M., and Diana Elrod, Massachusetts Avenue Commercial District, Indianapolis, Indiana, National Register of Historic Places Inventory–Nomination Form, 1981.

Kouwnhoven, John. A., *Made in America* (New York: Doubleday), 1948.

——, *Half a Truth Is Better than None* (Chicago: University of Chicago Press), 1982.

Kramp, Deborah J., Paramount Theatre, Aurora, Illinois, National Register of Historic Places Inventory–Nomination form, 1979.

——, Aurora Elks Lodge #705, Aurora, Illinois, National Register of Historic Places Inventory-Nomination Form, 1979.

Kreger, Janet L., Bay County Building, Bay City, Michigan, National Register of Historic Places Inventory-Nomination Form., 1981.

Kroeber, A. L., *The Arapaho* (Omaha: University of Nebraska Press), 1983.

Kubly, Vincent F., *The Louisiana Capitol: Its Art and Architecture* (Gretna, Louisiana: Pelican Publishing Company), 1995.

Lampert, Donald K., and John V. Corliss, Balban & Katz Oriental Theatre, National Register of Historic Places Inventory-Nomination Form, 1977.

Latham, Charles Jr., "Madame C.J. Walker & Company," *Traces of Indiana and Midwestern History*, Summer,1989, pp. 29–37.

Lifka, Mary Lauranne, The Mundelein College Skyscraper Building, Chicago, Illinois, National Register of Historic Places Inventory–Nomination Form, 1979.

Luebke, Frederic C., ed., *A Harmony of the Arts: The Nebraska State Capitol* (Lincoln, Nebraska: University of Nebraska Press), 1990.

Lynd, Robert S., and Helen Merrell Lynd, *Middletown: A Study in American Culture* (New York: Harcourt, Brace and Company), 1929.

——, *Middletown in Transition* (New York: Harcourt, Brace and Company), 1937.

Marsden, Michael T., and Jack Nachbar, "The Indian in the Movies," *Handbook of North American Indians* (Washington: Smithsonian Institution), 1988.

McCullough, J. Bernard, Madame C. J. Walker Building, Indianapolis, Indiana, National Register of Historic Places Inventory–Nomination Form, 1979.

McGee, W. J., "The Siouan Indians," *Bureau of American Ethnology* (Washington, D.C.: Government Printing Office) 15th ed., 1897.

Meacham, Maryjo, First National Bank Building, Oklahoma City, Oklahoma, National Register of Historic Places Registration Form, 1990.

Menton, Theodore, *The Art Deco Style* (New York: Dover Publications), 1972.

Mooney, James, *The Ghost Dance Religion and the Souix Outbreak of 1890*, 14th Annual Report, Bureau of American Ethnology, Smithsonian Institution, Washington, D.C., 1892–93.

Moore, Patricia Anne, *The Casino: Avalon, Santa Catalina Island, California* (Avalon: Catalina Island Museum Society), 1979.

Morrison, Hugh, *Louis Sullivan: Prophet of Modern Architecture* (New York: W. W. Norton & Company), 1962.

Mumford, Lewis, *The Culture of Cities* (New York: Harcourt Brace Jovanovich, Inc.), 1970.

——, Ed., *Roots of Contemporary American Architecture* (New York: Dover Publications, Inc.), 1972.

Onderdonk, Francis S., Jr., *The Ferro-Concrete Style: Reinforced Concrete in Modern Architecture* (New York: Architectural Book Publishing Co.), 1928.

Park, Edwin Avery, *New Backgrounds for a New Age*, (New York: Harcourt, Brace), 1927.

Parks, Janet, and Alan G. Neumann, *The Old World Builds the New: The Guastavino Company and the Technology of the Catalan Vault, 1885–1962* (New York: Avery Architectural and Fine Arts Library and the Mirium and Ira Wallach Art Gallery at Columbia University in the City of New York), 1996.

Pehnt, Wolfgang, *Expressionist Architecture* (London: Thames & Hudson), 1973.

Peisch, Mark. L., *The Chicago School of Architecture: Early Followers of Sullivan and Wright* (New York: Random House), 1964.

——, Research files in Avery Library, Columbia University containing correspondence with Prairie school architects, their friends, associates, and relatives.

Pildas, Ave, *Art Deco Los Angeles* (New York: Harper & Row), 1979.

Prucha, Francis Paul, "United States Indian Policies, 1815–1860," *Handbook of North American Indians* (Washington: Smithsonian Institution), 1988.

Purcell, W. G., "Biographical Notes," October 1954, Avery Library, Columbia University.

Qualey, Carlton C., ed., *Thorstein Veblen* (New York: Columbia University Press), 1968.

Rathbun, Peter, and Charles Kirchner, Hyde Park Apartment Hotels, Chicago, Illinois, National Register of Historic Places Inventory–Nomination Form, 1985.

Robinson, Cervin, and Rosemarie Haag Bletter, *Skyscraper Style* (New York: Oxford University Press), 1975.

Rooney, William A., *Architectural Ornamentation in Chicago* (Chicago: Chicago Review Press), 1984.

Schleier, Merrill, *The Skyscraper in American Art, 1890–1931* (New York: Da Capo Press), 1986.

Schnorrenberg, John M., *Remembered Past, Discovered Future: The Alabama Architecture of Warren Knight & Davis, 1906–1961* (Birmingham: Birmingham Museum of Art), 1999.

Sexton, R. W., *American Commercial Buildings of Today* (New York: Architectural Book Publishing Company), 1928.

——, *The Logic of Modern Architecture* (New York: Architectural Book Publishing Company), 1929.

Shand, Phillip M., *Modern Picture Houses and Theaters* (Philadelphia: J. B. Lippincott), 1930.

Short, C. W., and R. Stanley-Brown, *Public Buildings: A Survey of Architecture of Projects Constructed by Federal and Other Governmental Bodies between the Years 1933 and 1939* (Washington D.C.: U.S. Government Printing Office), 1939.

Sinkevitch, Alice, ed., *AIA Guide to Chicago*, (New York: Harcourt Brace & Company), 1993.

Sloan, John, and Oliver LaFarge, *Introduction to American Indian Art* (Glorieta, New Mexico: The Rio Grande Press, Inc.), reprint of 1931 ed., 1973.

Small, Nora Pat, Terminal Building, Coffeyville, Kansas, National Register of Historic Places Inventory–Nomination Form, 1982.

Socolofsky, Homer E., and Huber Self, *Historical Atlas of Kansas* (Norman, Oklahoma: University of Oklahoma Press), 1972.

Stadler, Roberta, Reebie Storage and Moving Company, Chicago, Illinois, National Register of Historic Places Inventory–Nomination Form, 1978.

Starr, Kevin, *Material Dreams: Southern California Through the 1920s* (New York: Oxford University Press), 1990.

Sullivan, Donald, and Brian Danforth, *Bronx Art Deco Architecture*, Unpublished Manuscript, Graduate Program in Urban Planning, Hunter College, City University of New York, 1976.

Sullivan, Louis H., *Kindergarten Chats and Other Writings* (New York: Dover Publications, Inc.), 1979.

Tigerman, Stanley, *Chicago Architects: documenting the exhibit of the same name organized by . . .* (Chicago: The Swallow Press), 1976.

Troy, Nancy J., *Modernism and the Decorative Arts in France: Art Noveau to Le Corbusier* (New Haven: Yale University Press), 1991.

Tuchman, Maurice, ed., *The Spiritual in Art: Abstract Painting 1890–1985* (New York: Los Angeles County Museum of Art/Abeville Press), 1986.

Twombly, Robert, *Louis Sullivan: His Life and Work* (New York: Viking Penguin), 1986.

Vlack, Don, *Art Deco Architecture in New York* (New York: Harper & Row), 1974.

Voegelin, Erminie Wheeler, *Anthropological Report of the Ottawa, Chippewa, and Potawatomi Indians* (New York: Garland Publishing), 1974.

Washburn, Wilcomb E., volume editor, "History of Indian-White Relations," *Handbook of North American Indians* (Washington, D.C.: Smithsonian Institution), 1988.

Webb, Walter Prescott, *The Great Plains* (Lincoln: University of Nebraska Press), 1981.

Whiffen, Marcus, and Carla Breeze, *Pueblo Deco: The Art Deco Architecture of the Southwest* (Albuquerque: University of New Mexico Press), 1983.

Willensky, Elliot, and Norval White, eds., *AIA Guide to New York City* (New York: Harcourt Brace Jovanovich) 3d ed., 1988.

Wilson, Richard Guy, and Sidney K. Robinson, *The Prairie School in Iowa* (Ames: The Iowa State University Press), 1977.

Wright, Frank Lloyd, *The Natural House* (New York: Horizon Press), 1954.

Writers' Program of the WPA in the State of Kansas, *The WPA Guide to 1930s Kansas* (Lawrence: University of Kansas Press), 1984.

Writers' Program of the WPA in the State of Oklahoma, *The WPA Guide to 1930s Oklahoma* (Lawrence: University of Kansas Press), 1986.

Yanul, Thomas G., and Paul E. Sprague, Pickwick Theater Building, National Register of Historic Places Inventory–Nomination Form, 1974.

For further bibliographic information, please see
www.wwnorton.com/catalog/fall02/001970.htm

INDEX

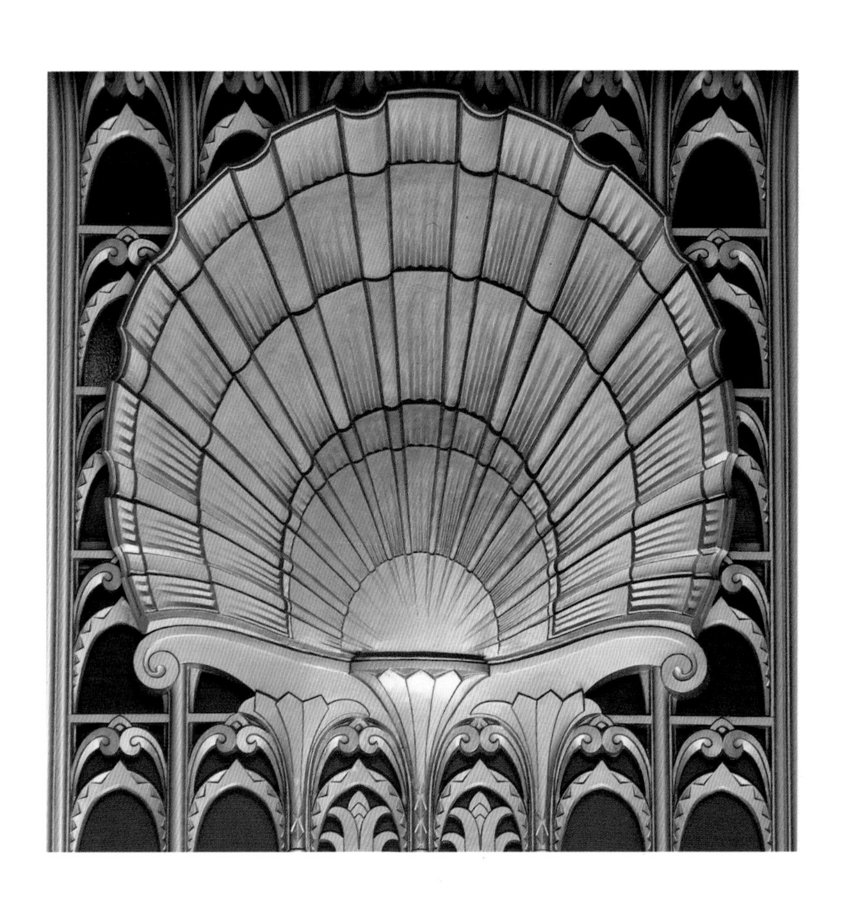